Yes!

Committed Beyond Choice, Even If...

By

Gary E. Wright

Wright Stuff Publishing

Amazon 2023

I am very grateful for the wonderful help of those on our team who worked to make this book possible.

Graphic Design: Rachel Ferguson, Mike Dalka

Cover Artwork: Parker Willits

Cover Design and Production: Mike Dalka

Editing: Rachel Ferguson, Carol Wright

Discussion Questions: Carol Wright

Dr. Gary E. Wright

206 S 850 E.

Greenfield, Indiana, 46140   317 513 9042

Referrals

"Listen to a wise man...and you hear distilled wisdom that can be applied to any life at any time. When Dt. Gary Wright speaks or writes; we have the privilege of listening to a wise man. His latest book is full of concise, Biblical, practical, applicable distilled wisdom. I especially appreciate how he writes from his own experiences as well as capturing the distilled wisdom of those he's learned from. As he writes about the essential experience of the Spirit-filled life—one of power, holy love, joy, fruitfulness, and Christlikeness—my heart burns with passionate agreement. As you listen to Gary's distilled wisdom, may your heart burn with passionate agreement, too!"

Dr. Tim Roehl, President, Fit & Flourish Network
Author of "TransforMissional Coaching", "Lead by Listening",
"Game Plan: Developing Intentional Missional Ministry" and "Fit & Flourish: Discovery How God Created
You to Make a Difference".

"Full surrender. The fullness of the Holy Spirit. Baptism with the Holy Spirit. Regardless of the terminology, the message in this work by Gary Wright is clear, convicting, and desperately needed in the times in which we live. Based on his own journey and numerous experiences as a pastor, evangelist, and revivalist, Gary Wright has put into everyday language the results of continuously saying 'Yes' to God. I highly recommend this enthralling work to every pastor and layman who are God chasers."

D Dennis. Engbrecht, PhD
Senior Vice President Emeritus
Bethel University (IN)

Loved this book! With personal story telling, incisive biblical examples, and a lifetime of ministry experience, Dr. Wright shares the key to fruitful and effective service for Christ whether you are in full time ministry or serving in any capacity. Chock full of wisdom and fire!

Pastor Matt Wickham
Brandywine Community Church

4

"In this present age when it seems that compromise and lukewarmness is the order of the day, Gary Wright's new book about radical commitment is a breath of fresh air. A much-needed read."

Lawrence Chewning
Musician/Composer "The Anchor Holds"

Dr. Gary Wright is a storyteller. That's no wonder; his stories capture the essence of the Master Story-teller, Jesus Christ. One of the things that has impressed me about Dr. Wright's preaching stories is the simple, yet profound transparency that lets the listener in on his own shortcomings. Such candid truths allow for every hearer to immediately connect to the message. That transparency is also masterfully captured for the reader in Dr. Wright's books.

"YES! Committed Beyond Choice, Even If..." displays something I believe is missing in many people's lives in the modern era; a simple legacy (a personal story) that has been passed from one generation to the next with the expectancy and challenge for the reader to assimilate into their own story. That which makes the reading such a blessing is the fact that Dr. Wright's candid journey is like our own and yet at the same time a challenge to understand how we too can rise above defeat and ultimately be in receipt of God's blessing again.

Pastor Terry Knighten
New Life Community Church
415 Mica Road Ridgeway, VA 24148
nlccalive.org

Dr. Wright's book is a joyful light in a world filled with overwhelming circumstances and obstacles. Yes buoys our spirits and empowers us to look to heaven for strength as we embrace the challenges of serving Christ, the Divine Yes, and fearlessly minister to those around us. This book is a call to action for every servant of Christ, especially those called to preach the Gospel. It speaks not only to the power of the Living God but to His desire to fill us with His Spirit and empower us to boldly proclaim His message of hope to our broken world. It is for love that the book was written and God's message shines through ... accept God's restorative grace, embrace the indwelling Christ, and walk as a bold warrior for the King of Kings. It is honest, pure, hope-filled, tender, personal, and convicting.

Angie Wetmore, MS IDT
Dean, Barclay College Online

Twenty-one years ago, Gary led me to the Lord. Prior to that day I did not believe in God. Since then, I have had the privilege to travel with him and share my testimony on several occasions. It is during our travel time that I experienced Gary's "Committed Beyond Choice" decisions for the Lord. He sometimes confesses a struggle he may have or has dealt with and then shares the outcome, always a changed heart. Other times it may be some discovery concerning quirks or tendencies the various individuals or people groups in the Bible possess. And most important to him is continuing to learn how Jesus did it.

I love those trips. Every time I spend a few days with Gary my spirit is refilled, and I can feel the glow of the Lord radiating out. Gary is the person in my life that closest resembles the heart of Jesus. As I read this book, I relive those road trips and beam again. Now you have an opportunity to experience the journey too. I love this book. Can't wait to facilitate a small group using it.

Wayne Phelps
CEO of Bula Forge & Machine, Inc. Cleveland, Ohio
Chairman of the Board, Friends of Recovery, Northeastern Ohio
Chairman of the Board, Friends of Recovery, Indiana
Elder of Friends Church Willoughby Hills, Ohio
Member of the Board, World Renewal

Table of Contents

Dedication

I have so enjoyed meeting people at an altar of prayer after this half-century plus of preaching and giving witness to Jesus. I am reminded of all the altar experiences when the Lord challenged us all to be totally committed to the Person of Jesus Christ, the Anointed One. Many deep friendships have been developed from these altars of surrender moments when someone, maybe you, said, "Yes!" to Him in the deepest way you could at that moment. This book, which required over a half-century of "walking" with Him to write, is dedicated to all of you I have met at the altar of being "Committed Beyond Choice."

Dr. Gary E. Wright

Forward

Twenty-one years ago, Gary led me to the Lord. Prior to that day I did not believe in God. Since then, I have had the privilege to travel with him and share my testimony on several occasions. It is during our travel time that I experienced Gary's "Committed Beyond Choice" decisions for the Lord.

He sometimes confesses a struggle he may have or has dealt with and then shares the outcome, always a changed heart. Other times it may be some discovery concerning quirks or tendencies the various individuals or people groups in the Bible possess. And most important to him is continuing to learn how Jesus did it.

I love those trips. Every time I spend a few days with Gary my spirit is refilled, and I can feel the glow of the Lord radiating out. Gary is the person in my life that closest resembles the heart of Jesus. As I read this book, I relive those road trips and beam again. Now you have an opportunity to experience the journey too. I love this book.

Can't wait to facilitate a small group using it.

Wayne Phelps

CEO & Founder of Bula Forge & Machine, Inc. Cleveland, Ohio

Chairman of the Board, Friends of Recovery, Northeastern Ohio

Chairman of the Board, Friends of Recovery, Indiana

Elder of Friends Church Willoughby Hills, Ohio

Member of the Board, World Renewal Greenfield, Indiana

Introduction
Yes? or No?

"There's a way of life (way, path or choice) that looks harmless enough (to man, woman, we humans); but...."

Proverbs 14:12 MSG[1]

Have you ever said "No," to God? Are you saying "Yes "to Him right now? Most of you reading this book have said "Yes," to Jesus. However, for most part, that means we were confused in our choices and finally admitted we needed something other than our original or amended plan. Maybe we had made a mess of things. For others, "mess" is too strong. Things were not working out like we thought they would. Someplace, we finally admitted we were unsure what to do next, so we asked for His help. We prayed to a Higher Power. As Kenneth Baily said, like a lost sheep, we reached a point where we were willing to be found by the Good Shepherd.

I'll be honest. I do not recall ever forming the thought in my brain, "No, God. I will not do it." That is a bit too much of a direct rejection of God for me. My "No's" have been a little more slippery or sneaky, less obvious to me. I grew up with Godly parents and grandparents. I grew up with absolute right and wrong. A direct "NO!" to the Almighty just seems too much. If I was going to do evil, it needed to be behind the authorities' back, out of eyesight. My rejection of Him has been more of the "apple in the garden" variety. Like Eve, she saw it, desired it, ate it, and sinned, then passed her sin to her husband. I was usually hoping no one else saw. For me, He had written, either in His Word, the Bible, or "written it on my heart," that it is wrong, a sin, and I chose to do it anyway. That has been my life pattern; I say "No," by my choices, not by actually forming the word in my mind. Do the sin. Hopefully, later, He will forgive. It's still a rejection of Him and His way. Somehow, it feels like a "lesser" sin at the time.

---

[1] (way, path or choice) are my own.

"One day long ago, God's Word came to Jonah, Amittai's son: "Up on your feet and on your way to the big city of Nineveh! Preach to them. They're in a bad way, and I can't ignore it any longer." But Jonah got up and went the other direction to Tarshish, running away from God." Jonah 1:1 MSG

Yes, I have done that too. I sense God wants me to do something, and I "went in the other direction." I may have just done nothing. I do not want to admit it's really...., Him. Here, it says, "running away from God."

Now, most of us rejecting, ignoring, or running from God do not get swallowed by the "huge fish" we usually have circumstances or people in our lives that encourage right or godly behavior and choices. "Then God assigned a huge fish to swallow Jonah. Jonah was in the fish's belly three days and nights."[2] Here we go! Someone or something "on assignment" from G.O.D., Himself! Yes! I've been there, done that! Early in my life, that would have been Dad. As I struggled with proper behavior as a teen, spending the day with my earthly father was not always among the Top Ten things I wanted to do. He was a pastor, evangelist, really a revivalist. More importantly, my dad was Godly. Jesus dwelled and lived in him richly. Jesus just seemed to ooze from every pore of his body. If one was struggling with sin, it was not fun to be around him. "Denzel Washington said, "Some people will never like you because your spirit irritates their demons."[3] Yeah, dad could be irritating and never say a word. It was more of who he <u>was,</u> not what he said. Although, what came out of his mouth could be irritating too.

He was a singer and whistler all day long! For most of Dad's life as a minister, like most preachers, he had to have another job, another vocation. Most of his ministry positions did not bring enough income to support our family. For example, his first pastorate, the year I was born, paid $5 a week. He had

---

[2] Jonah 1:17 MSG
[3] www.facebook.com post

to have another income. He taught himself to be a stone, brick, and block mason, then a general construction contractor. I started going to work with him before grade school and learned those trades too. All day long, Dad would lay stones, bricks, or blocks in construction, singing at the top of his lungs! He sang about Jesus. Sometimes, Dad made up his own lyrics when he forgot the original. He was deeply in love with Jesus. Dad constantly recited the story of the night Jesus found him. It was like he never got over it, Jesus saving him. However, when you're a teenager, this is not cool. When you were a teenager struggling with sin, his singing and occasionally whistling in between songs or as a part of it was not cool! He was my "huge fish." My father helped many people. However, he realized, seemingly from the beginning, he was "on assignment" with his three sons. He helped me; Jesus in him irritated me to do right and not do wrong.

Nevertheless, I need more than a human "huge fish" to be the best version of me. However, I think I am being truthful in saying that I thank the Lord every day for my godly, Spirit-filled, Jesus' oozing dad, Eugene "Gene" Wright. It took what happened to me at the Asbury Revival of 1970 to realize what a magnificent gift of God to me my parents were.

My mother was devoted to teaching me God's word by reading to me stories of children making Jesus-type decisions and choices. She started long before I attended school with these Jesus' story hours. She was quiet and shy, and emotionally fragile. However, she was bold and determined to teach me about Jesus through the story. I have been given much, and much shall be required before Christ.

"Remember, it is a sin to know what you ought to do and then not do it." James 4:17 NLT. Reading James always gets me in trouble. Jonah knew what to do and literally ran from it. Too often, I have too. "I know that all God's commands are spiritual, but I'm not. Isn't this also your experience?"........What I don't understand about myself is that I decide one way, but then I act another, doing things I absolutely despise. So, if I can't

be trusted to figure out what is best for myself and then do it....
I need something more! For if I know the law but still can't keep
it, and if the power of sin within me keeps sabotaging my best
intentions, I obviously need help! I realize that I don't have what
it takes. I can will it, but I can't do it. I decide to do good, but I
don't really do it; I decide not to do bad, but then I do it
anyway. My decisions, such as they are, don't result in actions.
Something has gone wrong deep within me and gets the better
of me every time."[4] Yes, the Apostle Paul is right, "I need
something more!"

Here is my problem, my challenge. I'm a dad of four
children, plus spouses. In this writing, I have eight
grandchildren. I love my grandkids! We should have had them
first! I want them all, my family, to be blessed by God. I have
been so blessed. Without my parents' example and how as a
male, my dad had Jesus, I wouldn't be writing this book. I would
not have anything to write after this "Yes" or "No" Introduction.
Why? Because "There's a way of life (way, path, choices), that
(seems right or) looks harmless enough(to man, woman, we
humans); look again—it leads straight to hell....those people
(often) appear to be having a good time, but all that laughter
will end in heartbreak."[5] My, our, way is not good enough. Yes,
Jesus died on the cross. Yes, I asked Jesus to forgive my sins.
Yes, He forgave and forgives my sin. Unfortunately, I can still,
and do, mess it up. He is sufficient, and I am not. Me and my
family, need something more.

Reflection and Discussion Questions

1. Introduce yourself to the group by sharing your name, family,
what brought you to this study and your challenge to grow with
this study.

---

[4] Romans 7:14-20 MSG.
[5] Proverbs 14:12 MSG plus my own (translation).

2. Who was the first person who "reflected" Jesus to you? Give an example of what that looked like and why it spoke Jesus to you.

3. The Holy Spirits speaks to our spirit through personal thoughts and 'feelings' along with the Scripture. Which 'voice' do you place more important and why?

4. Do you have a memory of a time in your life when you know the Lord showed you the path and you struggled with that path? Please share what you are comfortable with.

Notes

_____
_____
_____
_____
_____
_____
_____
_____
_____
_____
_____

Chapter One
Committed Beyond Choice...Even if.

When God has all of you, then you have all of Him, and in Him there is perfect security.

E. Stanley Jones

I have a hard time remembering people's names. Do you have that problem? I am also amazed at what names I, we, do remember. I'll show you what I mean. I think I can give you two names, and you can fill in the blank on the third one. Shadrach, Meshach..... and? Billy Goat (Abednego). Amazingly, we remember those three culturally irrelevant names. I mean, how many times do you use the name Shadrach, Meshach, and Abednego? We don't use those names. By the way, those are not Hebrew names of the Old Testament, Greek names, or Aramaic of the New Testament. They are Babylonian. So, at lunch today, you can tell folks, "Do you know I speak Babylonian?" Shadrach, Meshach, and Abednego, probably Jewish teenagers, or early 20s, college-age at most, were taken out of their homes as prisoners, enslaved, kidnapped, and taken to the Babylonian King's court. Th King was a guy with a tricky name, Nebuchadnezzar. The three young Jewish men were trained to serve the Babylonian government. However, the king did something that they couldn't agree with, and they took their stand literally. The King made this golden statue "on the plain of Dura in the province of Babylon," he proclaimed that everybody "when you hear the sound of the horn, pipe, lyre, trigon, harp, dulcimer or bagpipe, and every kind of music, you are to fall down and worship the golden image that King Nebuchadnezzar has set up,"[6] in other words, worship this "it." We do not know if the three teenage boys went there intentionally to take their stand. We do know they decided not to bow to that idol. There were those, I am sure, who were jealous of their position of being trained with the very best educators and all that came with them being in the King's court. They turned them in. They squealed on them!

---

[6] Daniel 3 AMPC

"Therefore, at that time certain men of Chaldean descent came near and brought [malicious] accusations against the Jews. They said to King Nebuchadnezzar, 'O king, live forever! You, O king, have made a decree that every man who hears the sound of the horn, pipe, lyre, trigon, harp, dulcimer or bagpipe, and every kind of music shall fall down and worship the golden image, And that whoever does not fall down, and worship shall be cast into the midst of a burning fiery furnace. There are certain Jews whom you have appointed and set over the affairs of the province of Babylon—Shadrach, Meshach, and Abednego. These men, O king, pay no attention to you; they do not serve your gods or worship the golden image which you have set up." Daniel 3:8-12 AMPC

So, the trio of teenagers end up before the king. Now, the King is in an awkward spot. He and his leaders have chosen these three young men to be trained because of their intelligence, attractive looks, and their giftedness. Awkwardly, the three have gone against his national decree. However, the King wants to give them another chance. "Now, if you are ready when you hear the sound of the horn, pipe, lyre, trigon, harp, dulcimer or bagpipe, and every kind of music to fall down and worship the image which I have made, very good. But if you do not worship, you shall be cast at once into the midst of a burning fiery furnace, and who is that god who can deliver you out of my hands?"[7] What is their response? It is awesome! "Shadrach, Meshach, and Abednego answered King Nebuchadnezzar, "Your threat means nothing to us. If you throw us in the fire, the God we serve can rescue us from your roaring furnace and anything else you might cook up, O king. But even if he doesn't, it wouldn't make a bit of difference, O king. We still wouldn't serve your gods or worship the gold statue you set up."[8] The brash Jewish trio stated that they do not need to discuss it among themselves. They have already made and are committed to their choice, "Read our lips, no way, we are not going to bow!" We believe,

---

[7] Ibid. Verse 15
[8] Daniel 3 MSG

"The God we serve will rescue us…. but even if He does not…..we will not bow."

Never underestimate Spirit-filled, committed youth. There is a reason that God sent most revivals in North American history to the college campus. Check out the landscape of these movements of God, Asbury 1970, 2023, the Haystack Prayer meeting, and the Jesus Revolution. This age group does shake the gates of hell! They do make decisions that result in them being world changers. Dr. Dennis Kinlaw, President of Asbury College when revival came to Asbury in 1970, said:

"The power of (college) students committed to Christ has been made evident. The world has watched while other students have brought down administrations and shaken national governments. We have come to regard students as political and social revolutionaries. Now, God has let us see their potential as Christians. The young people in this (revival) movement have been the key. Faculty and administrators have been chauffeurs and guides while the Spirit has used the young to open closed doors and storm the enemy's bastions. This should really be no surprise. History reminds us that in 1806 it was two college sophomores and three freshmen at Williams College who triggered the movement of Christian missions in American life – a movement of God hardly surpassed elsewhere in Christian history. The major Christian movements of the 20th century – from independent faith missions to modern ecumenical movement – began in student groups in the late 19th century. Luther Wishard persuaded D. L. Moody to give four weeks in July of 1886 to college students. Few realized that history was being made. But from that group of 251 collegians who met with Moody came a movement of the Spirit that produced John R. Mott, Robert Speer, Samuel Zwemer, E. Stanley Jones, Wascom Pickett, the Student Volunteer Movement, the

20th century missionary thrust around the world, and laid the foundations of the ecumenical movement."[9]

Now, back to our story. These three young Jewish men made some advanced, pre-meditated decisions. "Notice, it says, "but even if He (God) does not rescue us." They had talked about this. "Our God is bigger than you," I ask you. What kind of attitude are they exhibiting here? John Maxwell calls this attitude an "I don't have to survive until tomorrow attitude." We are talking about the most powerful man in the world, King Nebuchadnezzar! Yet here they are singing the "My God is bigger than your God song!" I call it something else. I call it a "Committed Beyond Choice Attitude." Have you heard that descriptive attitude phrase before? Probably not. I made it up.[10] I labeled this approach because it is such a powerful pre-meditated attitude. When humans take this "I don't have to survive until tomorrow" approach, defeating position is difficult. In war or terrorism, those who are willing to give up their lives for their cause to accomplish a purpose, that act is often unstoppable. Suicide warriors are hard to stop. The choice is made, "Yes, I am willing to give up my life to make this happen!" The terrible 9/11 terrorists gave their lives for their cause, and others chose to give their lives to stop them and to save others, "Let's roll." Either way, it is a powerful attitude and approach. The Apostle Paul "And so, dear brothers and sisters, I plead with you to give your bodies to God because of all he has done for you. Let them be a living and holy sacrifice—the kind He will find acceptable. This is truly the way to worship Him."[11] That "Give up my life" attitude has often been a death outcome for Christians and others. Usually, it is an approach decided in advance, "Committed Beyond the Choice," of yes or no. It is a commitment to God, saying "YES" to Him and His agenda. The "Yes" or "No" has been made ahead of the outcome. That is *Committed Beyond Choice*.

Shadrach, Meshach and Abednego were *Committed Beyond the Choice* of yes or no. Their premeditated answer was to God: "Yes "to

---

[9] https://goodnewsmag.org/gn-archive-and-suddenly-god-was-with-us/
[10] I think I first heard my friend Edwin Cain call it that decades ago. Neither of us are certain.
[1111] Romans 12:1 NLT

God, "No," to King Neb. Throughout the Bible, there is One who constantly demonstrates "Yes." The Apostle Paul describes it this way, "The divine "Yes" has, at last, sounded in him, (Jesus) who affirms all of God's promises." The "Divine Yes" is Jesus, Himself, who said "Yes" to the cross. Everything about Jesus was "Yes!" to His Heavenly Father. Jesus said "Yes" to the humiliation of the cross. It is Jesus who, by choice, died and rose again, which is the resounding "Yes" of all times. Let me tell you, when young men and women, or anyone else, is like these three, when a human being is Committed Beyond Choice in "Yes" to God and combining with the "Divine Yes" Himself, there has been historically, some kind of spiritual combustion in the realms of heaven that shake the gates of hell! Sometimes those gates swing right open for Peter, Paul, and Silas! I confess until I read the great missionary to India, E. Stanley Jones' final book, "The Divine Yes," I had not noticed 2 Corinthians 1:19-20, translated by Moffatt. "The Divine 'Yes' has at last been sounded in Him for in Him is the 'Yes' that affirms all the promises of God." The Asbury College alumnus, Dr. Jones, said we need the "Divine 'Yes' because humanity has sunk deeper and deeper into negativism."[12]

Now, King Nebuchadnezzar has a "tude." He is furious! "Nebuchadnezzar, his face purple with anger, cut off Shadrach, Meshach, and Abednego."[13] His attitude towards the three young men changed. In his moment of fury, the King commands the meanest, the baddest, most proficient soldiers he has, and unfortunately, they perish from the fire and heat, the furnace heated seven times hotter, themselves as they throw the three teens, "bound hand and foot, fully dressed from head to toe, were pitched into the roaring fire."

The next question is, what is God's response when He has Committed Beyond Choice believers who get in trouble because of that Committed Beyond Choice approach? I picture the king sitting in front of the blazing furnace. It's not going well for King Neb. He's having a bad day. He's having a horrible day. His elite, best soldiers are dead on the floor because of his egocentric choices. He apparently is sitting or standing, looking into the furnace wondering what just happened? The

---

[12] E. Stanley Jones. *The Divine Yes*. Nashville; Abingdon, 1975,26.
[13] Daniel 3 MSG.

room is scorching hot. It smells of burning fire and flesh. The King asked a question of the people that were there with him. "Suddenly, Nebuchadnezzar jumped up in amazement and exclaimed to his advisers, "Didn't we tie up three men and throw them into the furnace? " His advisors knew their roles and job descriptions. They all said, "Certainly, O king." That was their job, saying, "Yes!." "Look!" Nebuchadnezzar shouted. "I see four men, unbound, walking around in the fire unharmed! And the fourth looks like a god!" On this occasion, I believe that the Lord Jesus, the "Lord of Heaven's Armies," turned to the angels Gabriel and Michael and said, "Never mind, boys, I'm going to go take care of this one Myself!" Well, glory! When humans choose some holy challenge for God that is bigger than human ability, and they get in trouble for that Committed Beyond Choice endeavor, He will personally rescue us as He has promised. God says, "Do not be afraid, for I have ransomed you. I have called you by name; you are mine. When you go through deep waters, I will be with you. When you go through rivers of difficulty, you will not drown. When you walk through the fire of oppression, you will not be burned up; the flames will not consume you. For I am the Lord, your God,   the Holy One of Israel, your Savior......you are precious to me. You are honored, and I love you. Do not be afraid, for I am with you."[14] If you want to experience God, live a *Committed Beyond Choice* life for Christ. You <u>will</u> surely encounter the fiery furnace, the Daniel, and the lion's den-type challenges. Yes, you may become a martyr for Christ. His promises are not about your physical body and life but your heart. Your spiritual body.

Nevertheless, you will turn in the heat and fire of the furnace, or the breath of the lion is on you; you will turn and see Him who promises, "After you have suffered a while, I will personally come and pick you up and stand you firmly in place, and make you make you stronger than ever."[15] Those are the words of Simon Peter. What had he experienced? , "After you have suffered a while, I will personally come and pick you up." Remember Peter's words in John 21? "Yes, Lord. You know that I love you." "Yes," to the Lord is seldom an overnight sensation but a Christ-led process.

---

[14] Isaiah 43 NLT
[1515] 1 Peter 5: 10 TLB

As believers, God will challenge us to do something more significant than a human being can do. He challenges us, and if we're willing to go forward as *Committed Beyond Choice*, "Yes" Christ followers, like these three Jewish young men, then we will experience God. Why? Because we will need His miracle-working resurrection power or fall flat on our faces, and we will fail. This is how He brings glory to Himself and Christ-Confidence to us. We have decided in advance. The answer is, "Yes!"

Let me give you another example. The Apostle Paul, at the end of his ministry, asks in Acts 20 to travel and meet with the elders from the church at Ephesus. As they gathered, he said to them, "Compelled by the Spirit I'm going to Jerusalem, not knowing what will happen to me there. I only know that in every city the Holy Spirit warns me that prison and hardships are facing me. However, I consider my life worth nothing to me if only I can finish that task the Lord Jesus has given me, the task of testifying to the gospel of God's grace, and now, I know that none of you among whom I've gone about preaching the Kingdom will ever see me again."

I'm not sure if I was in prayer for today, which I have been, and the Lord spoke to me and said, "Now, if you do this next preaching assignment, they are going to arrest you, they're going to put you in jail, and they're going to beat you and whip you." I might say to the Lord, "Wow! Thank you, Lord, for warning me and taking care of me! I'll let him know I'm not coming. I'm going in another direction." Remember, that seems to be what concerned Jonah, so he "went in another direction." Look through Paul's words here; you do not get any of that here. He just says, "Yes, I'm going."

There were people in the Apostle Paul's day who dedicated themselves to stopping his ministry. Afterall, Paul was the iconic anti-Christianity guy turned Jesus Freak. If you were in a group of people that had the job of trying to stop the Apostle Paul, can you imagine how difficult that would have been? Imagine you're in this task force group meeting to stop the Apostle Paul from this "Jesus' revolution talk and movement. "The task force tells him, "Son, you have ignored our warnings about this Jesus Speak. If you don't stop,. we're going to whip you until you can't stand up." "There, that should do it!" they thought.

They bring in the ferocious soldier guy with the whip. He is a giant of a man standing there with his tool of torture and pain. Cruelly, he is making snapping sounds with the ugly leather whip. The whip, split into nine strips with bone and metal tied to the ends, is ready to tear into the prisoner's skin. I think I know what the Apostle Paul would say and do. I see Paul turn his back to the soldier with the whip. Paul slips down his cloak to show his back, which had been whipped so many times and so fiercely that the open wounds would never heal.

"I am trying to remember when the last time this happened?" Paul asks, thinking out loud. "I think the last time was at Philippi. That was a great day and night for the church and Jesus Christ. After they whipped me and my friend Silas, that jailor experienced a miracle. God showed up as Silas that night, and I sang songs to Jesus in the inner prison. An earthquake shook the jail, the prison doors flew open, and our chains fell off! It was awesome! Thinking all the prisoners had escaped, the jailer was about to take his own life before I stopped him. When prisoners escaped on his watch, the punishment for him would have had him stripped, his clothes tied around his feet then burned. He was choosing suicide from his own sword over this punishment. But I told him all were still there in jail. The Spirit of Jesus Himself had "personally come" and touched his mind and heart. That night he took Silas and me home with him. He fed us and dressed our wounds. He introduced us to all of his family. In turn, we introduced him, his family, and his whole household to the Lord Jesus. They all became followers of Jesus." Can you imagine the Apostle Paul smiling at the guy with the whip and saying, "Now, who will it be today? Who is going to whip me this time?" The task force decides, "We need to meet again."

So, they met again. They came out with sad faces and said, "You're really stubborn! We're just going to throw you in jail and throw away the key! We've had it with you!" Paul would have smiled and said, "That's just super fine! I'm quite familiar with your prison system. If you just let me know what prison you're placing me into, I'll let the brothers and sisters know I'm coming because we've had a great movement of the Spirit of Jesus sweep through the entire Roman prison system. Thank you! That will be great!" The task force looked at each other and said, "I think we need to meet again."

The anti-Paul task force meets one last time. They say, "He's given us no choice! "They come out in extreme frustration and anger and say, "You just won't keep your mouth shut about this Jesus thing. We are going to execute you! You are dead!" Here, I do not have to guess what Paul would say; I know what the Apostle Paul would say; I've read it. "Thank you! Thank You! This solves a big question for me. I was not sure which I should choose. I am pulled in two directions. I want very much to leave this life and be with Christ, which is a far better thing, but for the sake of believers, it is much more important that I remain alive."[16] "You are solving a great problem for me!" Should I go to heaven and be with Christ or stay here and work in the church? " For me to live is Christ [His life in me], and to die is gain [the gain of the glory of eternity]."[17] Amazing! *Committed Beyond Choice* soldiers of the cross are unstoppable! Only death stopped Paul. Well, not really. He wrote the majority of the most read and studied book in the world. The Anti-Paul movement failed. He said, "Five times I was given the thirty-nine lashes by the Jews; 25 three times I was whipped by the Romans; and once I was stoned. I have been in three shipwrecks, and once I spent twenty-four hours in the water. In my many travels I have been in danger from floods and from robbers, in danger from my own people and from Gentiles; there have been dangers in the cities, dangers in the wilds, dangers on the high seas, and dangers from false friends."[18] These confrontations only add to his credibility. When you consider the written pages he wrote of our New Testament, and we are still discussing him, did they stop him?

Of course, I've saved the best for last. I love this passage of Luke:13:31-32 NIV It says: "At that time some Pharisees came to Jesus and said to him, "Leave this place and go somewhere else. Herod wants to kill you." He (Jesus) replied, "Go tell that fox, 'I will keep on driving out demons and healing people today and tomorrow, and on the third day, I will reach my goal." If you didn't understand what Jesus was saying, let me put it in my Hoosier lingo. OK? The Pharisees said to Jesus, "You need to leave Jesus." These were Pharisees now! You often

---

[16][16] Philippians 1:23 GNT
[17] Philippians 3:21 AMPC
[18] 2 Corinthians 11:26 GNT

see them as Jesus' opponents but let me tell you they were the most spiritual people of his day, and so many of them, like you and me, when He (Jesus) came near them, fell in love with this Jesus! They are distraught. "Leave Jesus; Herod is coming to kill you!" Jesus' response? Translated into my Hoosier, "You tell that old fox," I like it already. "If he wants to find me, I'll be here all day today, healing the people and driving out the demons." And, if he doesn't get to it today..... I'll be here all day tomorrow healing the people driving out the demons.......and if he doesn't get around to it today or tomorrow, you tell that old fox, I'll be here all day the third day until I accomplish my goal of healing the people and driving out the demons! You tell that old fox!" Folks that is our leader! I don't know about you, but I feel like charging hell with a squirt gun!

If He is my leader, and He is, I want to be *Committed Beyond Choice*! I want to give it up for him every day. I want to say, "Yes!" I want to be challenged with situations beyond human abilities, things only He can do through me. I want to be able to experience God! That might include the fiery furnace, perhaps the lion's den. It could mean going through flood waters or the fire. What if I get in trouble because of that *Committed Beyond Choice* approach? I want Jesus to say, "Never mind Michael, never mind Gabriel, I'm going to take care of this Myself!" I say, "Glory!" That is one of the most glorious ways to experience God. Remember, Peter said, "After you have suffered a while, I (Jesus) will personally come and pick you up and stand you firmly in place, and make you make you stronger than ever." The Promise of His Presence, are you interested?

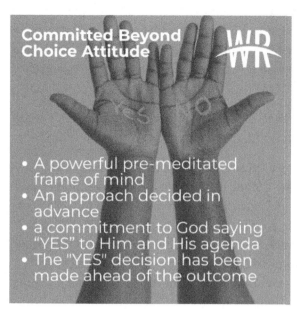

Committed Beyond Choice Attitude WIR

- A powerful pre-meditated frame of mind
- An approach decided in advance
- a commitment to God saying "YES" to Him and His agenda
- The "YES" decision has been made ahead of the outcome

Our communities need Jesus' miracles, and He's chosen us so that they can experience Jesus. I coached public school basketball. Sometimes in a game, your team gets tired or loses focus and discipline, and they don't want to make all the passes, or they don't want to make all the running cuts to get the open shots. At this point, they are often tempted to do the lazy, lack of commitment thing and just stand out there on the floor and shoot long 3's shot. They settle for just long shots that don't require running and extra passes. There are Christians who have settled in the same non-committal way. "OK, I'm saved. I'm going to heaven. Don't take this religious thing so seriously." That sounds like a recipe for purposelessness and boredom. That is not imitating Jesus as we are instructed to do.

The writer in the book of Hebrews made it clear, "We'd better get on with it. Strip down, start running—and never quit! No extra spiritual fat, no parasitic sins. Keep your eyes on Jesus, who both began and finished this race we're in. Study how he did it. Because he never lost sight of where he was headed—that exhilarating finish in and with God—he could put up with anything along the way: Cross, shame, whatever. And now he's there, in the place of honor, right alongside God. When you find yourselves flagging in your faith, go over that story again, item by item, that long litany of hostility he plowed through. That will shoot adrenaline into your souls!"[19]

---

[19] Hebrews 12 MSG

Therefore, if you want to experience Jesus, if you get a taste of him showing up in the middle of the fiery furnace, just because you are headed for heaven, hopefully, is not enough. Don't settle! Live with a purpose, His purpose for you. Say, "Yes!" Live *Committed Beyond Choice* to Jesus Christ.

What are the "Yes!" Next Steps for Living a *Committed Beyond Choice* for Jesus? Hebrews 12 gives instruction:

1. Focus on Jesus. "Keep your eyes on Jesus." How do you do that? "Study how He did it." "Go over that story again and again, item by item." I like to say, "Read the Red" in your red-letter editions of the Gospels of Matthew, Mark, Luke and John. For North Americans I recommend Eugene Peterson's "The Message" translation that I quoted Hebrews 12. It is an accurate translation and in the cultural vernacular of we North Americans. Notice how Jesus related to all peoples, how He talked acted, loved, cared.

2. Keep parasitic sin out of your life. The analogy here is that of a runner in an race and sin weights down the runner. Therefore, strip down and run, run away from sin and emulate the sinless Jesus.

3. Finish the race as He did. Never lose sight of where He is headed. His goals are our goals, let Him lead us. Plow through opposition.

4. Expect suffering, hostilities for a while. Remember Peter's words, "After you have suffered a while, He personally will come." "that exhilarating finish in and with God—he could put up with anything along the way: Cross, shame, whatever." Notice, "in and with God." We should expect Him to Come to our side when suffering.

5. Expect Him to increase your faith (flagging in your faith solution) and to "shoot spiritual adrenaline in your souls." And as Peter said, "pick you up (yes, we may have fallen or been knocked down), "and make us stronger.than ever." Say, "Yes!"

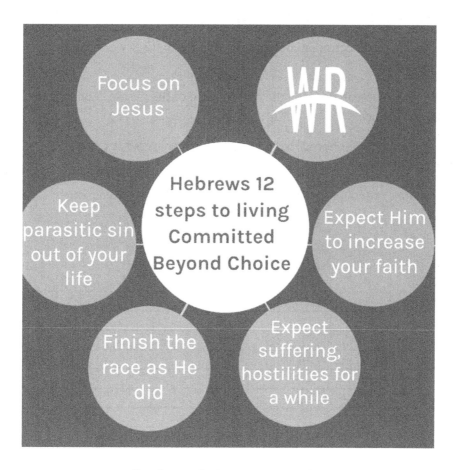

Focus on Jesus

Hebrews 12 steps to living Committed Beyond Choice

Keep parasitic sin out of your life

Expect Him to increase your faith

Finish the race as He did

Expect suffering, hostilities for a while

Reflection and Discussion Questions

1. Share a highlight from this past week, where did God show up in your life?

2. Which generation are you?

a. The Silent Generation: Born 1928–1945

b. Baby Boom Generation: Born 1946–1964

c. Generation X: Born 1965–1980

d. Millennial Generation or Generation Y: Born 1981–1996

e. Generation Z or iGen: Born 1997–2010

f. Generation Alpha: Born After 2000

3. What do you consider your generations strengths & weaknesses? Challenges?

4. How would you describe the author's use of the phrase "Committed Beyond Choice?"

4. Have you experienced that 'even if' event? Share what you gained from losing your agenda.

5. Share a 'need' to see more evidence of your 'even if' mindset.

Notes

_____

_____

_____

_____

_____

_____

_____

_____

_____

_____

_____

_____

_____

_____

_____

_____

_____

_____

Chapter Two
Awkward Obedience

Mary responded, "I am the Lord's servant. May everything you have said about me come true."

Luke 1:38 NLT

After saying these things, Jesus headed straight up to Jerusalem. When he got near Bethphage and Bethany at the mountain called Olives, he sent off two of the disciples with instructions: "Go to the village across from you. As soon as you enter, you'll find a colt tethered, one that has never been ridden. Untie it and bring it. If anyone says anything, asks, 'What are you doing?' say, 'His Master needs him.'" The two left and found it just as he said. As they were untying the colt, its owners said, "What are you doing untying the colt?" They said, "His Master needs him." Luke 11:28-34 MSG

It sounds simple, but it is not. It feels a bit scary, often complicated, and down to "Awkward!" Jesus picks and assigns two followers to get a donkey. It is the "Donkey Project." There is a problem; He does not own the donkey, and two of His students get it. It IS awkward. Will the owners accuse the two of stealing the donkey? Jesus tells them what to say, but... "If anyone says anything, asks, 'What are you doing?' say, 'His Master needs him." Needs it for what? Can you hear the two students of Jesus say to each other, "Why do we always get these "donkey jobs"? I imagine it just does not make sense to these two. One may have said, "I have a bad feeling about this." Have you ever found yourself in this kind of situation? Do you sense the Lord asking you to do something that doesn't make sense? Have you found yourself headed to that conversation thinking, "I have a bad feeling about this?" I confess to feeling I have had too many "donkey jobs"! How about you?

The Bible is full of these kinds of "awkward obedience" narratives. Is there any tougher example of "Awkward Obedience" in the Bible than, "Then God said (to Abraham), "Take your son, your only son, whom you love—Isaac—and go to the region of Moriah. Sacrifice him there as a burnt offering on a mountain I will show you." This story is so awkward for those of us who teach the scriptures; many ignore it. Sacrifice your child? Really? Notice there is no augment or alternative plan from Abraham, just obedience. "Early the next morning, Abraham got up and loaded his donkey." It is obvious, at this time in his life, Abraham was *Committed Beyond Choice*; his "Yes" response has previously been made. "Abraham took the wood for the burnt offering and placed it on his son Isaac, and he carried the fire and the knife. As the two of them went on together, Isaac spoke up and said to his father, Abraham, "Father?" "Yes, my son?" Abraham replied. "The fire and wood are here," Isaac said, "but where is the lamb for the burnt offering?" Abraham answered, "God himself will provide the lamb for the burnt offering, my son." And the two of them went on together."[20] Talk about awkward moments? "Daddy, where is the lamb for the burnt offering?"

Dr. Dennis Kinlaw, President of Asbury College during the 1970 Revival, describes God's foundation approach to these moments. "Mount Moriah as Abraham raised the knife to kill Isaac, when God's angel stopped him, saying, "Abraham, do not touch the lad." I heard the second Person of the Trinity say to the first Person, "Father, we are coming back here someday, aren't we?" And the Father said, "Yes, in about nineteen hundred years." "The next time it won't be one of them on the altar, will it?" I heard the Son ask. "No," the Father said. "The next time you will be there." "Father, when the Roman soldiers are about to put the spikes through my hands and feet, will you say, 'Do not touch the

---

[20] Genesis 22 NIV.

lad'?" And I thought I heard the Father say, "No, Son. We never ask them to do in symbol what we have not done in reality." Abraham sacrificed everything he had to become the intermediary between God and the nations. This is why Abraham is our model of faith. Jesus is the ultimate illustration of what God called Abraham to do: Jesus emptied himself of position, possessions, and all that he had, in order to be our Priest. If God called Abraham to do what he called his Son to do, does he not call us to do the same?"[21] Kinlaw says these "Awkward Moments" are about faith. Jesus is our example.

Did Abraham feel awkward when he explained to Sarah that they had to move, but he had no clue where to? They would learn where they were moving to as they were moving. That Abraham and Sarah's conversation had to be awkward for that husband.

I understand Moses's question to God's sending him to tell Pharaoh to release the nation of Israel, "Please send someone else." He was 80 years old! Did he feel awkward each time he warned Pharaoh of the coming plagues? Pharoah was the most powerful man in the world!

How did Noah feel when his neighbors made fun of him and his Ark? Yeah, awkward! Walk through that Hebrews 11-chapter, *God's Hall of Faith,* and consider each person and ask, "How did they feel about the situations described to be their act of faith? Did it feel? Comfortable? In the next chapter of Hebrews, we find the description of our ultimate model and example.

> "Keep your eyes on Jesus, who both began and finished this race we're in. Study how he did it. Because he never lost sight of where he was headed—that exhilarating finish in and with God— he could put up with anything along the way:

---

[21] Kinlaw, Dennis. The Mind of Christ (p. 33). Warner Press. Kindle Edition.

Cross, shame, whatever." Hebrews 12:1 MSG. He could put up with anything, "Cross, shame." Was hanging naked on a cross awkward? Was being falsely accused of being a criminal awkward? Paul reminds us, "When the time came, he (Jesus) set aside the privileges of deity and took on the status of a slave, became human! Having become human, he stayed human. It was an incredibly humbling process. He didn't claim special privileges. He sat aside His superpowers. Instead, he lived a selfless, obedient life and then died a selfless, obedient death—and the worst kind of death at that—a crucifixion. Philippians 2:5 MSG

Some Donkey Jobs in the Bible:

WR

- **Disciples** getting the Donkey (Luke 11)
- **Abraham** offering Isaac (Genesis 22)
- **Moses** going to Pharoah (Exodus 4)
- **Noah** building the ark (Genesis 6)
- **Mary**, pregnant and unmarried (Matthew 1)
- **Naman** and the dirty river (2 Kings 5)
- **Ananias** helping Saul (Acts 9)

How convenient was it for Mary, mother of Jesus, to be found pregnant while engaged to Joseph? Was that awkward? Was it "awkward" for Joseph to be engaged to a pregnant woman that he knew he had never had a sexual relationship with? I could say that most relationships people have or have with Jesus Christ will result in an "awkward" event or situation requiring a decision that if we say "Yes" to it, the result is awkward obedience. The Apostle Paul comes out and says it. "Whatever God has promised gets stamped with the Yes of Jesus. In Him, this is what we preach and pray, the great Amen, God's Yes and our Yes together, gloriously evident. God affirms us, making us a sure thing in Christ, putting his Yes within us. By his Spirit, He has stamped us with his eternal pledge—a sure beginning of what He is destined to complete." Notice the "God's Yes and our Yes together, gloriously evident. God affirms us, making us a sure thing in Christ, putting his Yes within us. By his Spirit, he has stamped us." 2 Corinthians 1:20-22 MSG.

Jesus said "Yes!" to all the Father asked Him to do. He became the "Divine Yes!" Our job description is the same. Whatever He asks of us, we say "Yes!" The Bible examples seem to guarantee. However, this will lead to "Awkward Obedience" moments.

So, what does this "Awkward Obedience" look like today? What is it for you and me? I can tell you what it means for my wife and me. Early in my life, I felt God calling my wife and I to plant a new church in Traverse City, Michigan. We knew no one there. I had served as an evangelist, a revivalist that required all our faith. It was difficult for a newly married couple to live without a guaranteed income. We lived by faith on offerings and donations without knowing what was next. That, for us, was "Awkward Obedience." However, we found comfort and peace in seeing the Lord provide for us.

Nevertheless, about the time we developed the rhythm of trusting Him, He changed our directions. We lived on the farm

(Carol's parents had a vacant house), and it was spring, and the grass needed mowing. I went to buy a lawn mower at the local farm and lawn supply owned by Harry Cooper. Harry was a bi-vocational pastor and head of the outreach board of our denominational tribe. "Gary, would you ever consider pastoring?" "No," I replied. I was telling the truth. I loved the revivalistic evangelism work we were doing. It was hard, but seeing local churches experience stages of renewal and revival that led to their friends and family coming to Christ was so exciting.

Carol played the piano, I sang and preached. We added singers Dana Howard Russo, and Mike Breese, while Cliff "Doc" Moser did advance preparation work to form a great and talented team. We were still experiencing the Asbury/Anderson Revival era. (See my book, *He Just Showed Up: An Eyewitness to Revival.*)[22] It was a movement of the Holy Spirit. We saw a lot of fruit. We were booked up about one year in advance in churches and other events. We were just getting started. No, I was not interested in pastoring. "We need someone to start a new congregation in Traverse City, Michigan. We closed the old church, and we want to start over," Harry said. "Would you pray about it?" he asked. I said I would and left without a lawn mower.

Over the coming weeks, Carol and I began to hear the "Whisper" of the Spirit of Jesus to go to a city we had never been to, nor did we know anyone there. We visited Traverse City. We talked to Harry's board. At their request, we wrote a possible strategy to plant a new church congregation in the old, remodeled church. We accepted the invitation. We said a tearful and uneasy farewell to our team and supporters. It did feel awkward. It was outside our comfort zone.

We took the plunge and moved to a place where we had never been, other than our weekend visit, and knew no one. We

---

[22] Wright, Gary. *He Just Showed Up: An Eyewitness to Revival.* Amazon. 2021.

worked hard trying to find unchurched people who would consider being churched. Yes, again, awkward. One moment of that awkwardness stands out in my memory. We set an opening date for the first Sunday morning service. Carol and I had set aside some funds we had raised personally for advertising. I spent all of what was left on announcing our inaugural event. We purchased newspaper ads and sent 10,000 invitations. Even billboards were obtained. It was funds we had raised and not a denominational budget. I didn't have to ask anyone's permission. The day came February 1, 1976. All the work, all the conversations, and anticipation. Then it happened. That inaugural Sunday morning, we woke up to one of the worst snow blizzards we had ever experienced. I was the janitor and pastor. I headed out the door to shovel the snow from the church sidewalks and steps. I felt very lonely as I tried to scoop the blowing and blinding snow. I looked behind me, and the snow-filled where I had last shoveled. A voice in my head said, "Gary, what a fool you are! Today, and this whole project, will be a failure. You spent all your advertising money on this? God did not call you here to plant a new church! You were booked up in advance for a year! You made the wrong decision. What a fool you are!" It felt worse than awkward; I felt like a complete loser! I wasn't a pastor. I was an evangelist, a revivalist. Meanwhile, the blowing, drifting snow continued. "What a mess I have made!" I thought. Then there was that other Whisper. It included that inner spark of hope and energy. It gave me the courage to speak to the enemy. "If I am a fool, then I choose to be a fool for Jesus. I rebuke you in the name of Jesus!"

I shoveled and salted the walks and steps. Poorly I might add. Somehow, over 70 plus people attended that first Sunday! Some said they hit drifts of snow coming over the hoods of their cars going home that day. Traverse City had a snowfall of over 200 inches a year; they were well acquainted and prepared for significant snowfalls, but Carol and I were not. The old church sanctuary would be full of people seeking Christ in a short time. That "You fool!" awkward, depressing moment shoveling the blowing snow was almost fifty years ago as I write this. Nevertheless, I can take you to the exact spot on the sidewalk where I listened to the defeating words of my mind and the enemy. I am not the hero here. I was defeated. Then God. Then God rose, turned "awkward" defeat into hope, and changed lives.

When I read through that excellent faith chapter, Hebrews 11, and observed each person in God's "Hall of Faith," I noticed most people had to move geographically and were displaced outside their comfort zones. Noah, Abraham and, Sarah, Moses all had to move geographically. Something huge in our souls occurs when we pick up and move our home to some new place. It is usually a further step of faith that feels awkward. Israel, as a nation, was constantly displaced. Sometimes they moved by choice; other times, someone forced their movement. Our view as readers of the Bible is that God was always in control. I am confident that it did not feel that way to the people and leaders of Israel.

Just picking one in the "Hall of Faith," Noah, the entire story is chalked full of awkward moments and situations. Jesus verified the Noah story and described people's reaction to Noah, "The time of the Son of Man will be just like the time of Noah— everyone carrying on as usual, having a good time right up to the day Noah boarded the ship. They suspected nothing until the flood hit and swept everything away." Luke 17:26-27 MSG. I have often felt sorry for Noah and his family. It was the ultimate "Donkey" job description, literally. "It was by faith that Noah built a large boat to save his family from the flood. He obeyed God, who warned him about things that had never happened before." Hebrews 11:7 NLT. "Build a large boat from cypress wood and waterproof it with tar, inside and out. Then construct decks and stalls throughout its interior." Genesis 6 NLT. If you have ever visited the replica of the Ark in Kentucky, the USA, it was an enormous task for Noah and his family (only eight people). "Bring a pair of every kind of animal—a male and a female—into the boat with you to keep them alive during the flood." We think walking the dog is inconvenient!

Awkward Obedience examples in the Bible are not just for the biblically famous characters. We often focus on the big names. Naman " was a great man in the sight of his master and highly regarded because, through him, the Lord had given victory to Aram. He was a valiant soldier, but he had leprosy." In order to be healed from his leprosy, the prophet Elisha said through a messenger, "Go, wash yourself seven times in the Jordan, and your flesh will be restored and you will be cleansed."[23] However, Naaman finds this humiliating and way below his pay grade treatment. The Bible describes Naaman's rage and anger as he turns his chariot and goes the other way. But "Naaman's servants went to him and said, "My father, if the prophet had told you to do some great thing, would you not have done it? How much more, then, when he tells you, 'Wash and be cleansed'!" So, he went down and dipped himself in the Jordan seven times, as the man of God had told him, and his flesh was restored and became clean like that of a young boy." Awkward moments for Naaman? Yes, but what about the servants in this story? In the beginning of this story, the servant girl says, "I know someone who can heal my master." Then the servants interrupt Naaman's fit of anger with, "Give it a try." The servants are the real faith heroes of "Awkward Obedience." They took the risk for the well-being of someone else by putting their own lives on the line.

Finally, I point to a little story in the book of Acts. The focus is on Saul, who becomes the great Apostle Paul.

---

[23] 2 Kings 5 NIV.

" There was a disciple in Damascus by the name of Ananias. The Master spoke to him in a vision: "Ananias. "Yes, Master?" he answered. "Get up and go over to Straight Avenue. Ask at the house of Judas for a man from Tarsus. His name is Saul. He's there praying. He has just had a dream in which he saw a man named Ananias enter the house and lay hands on him so he could see again. "Ananias protested, "Master, you can't be serious. Everybody's talking about this man and the terrible things he's been doing, his reign of terror against your people in Jerusalem! And now he's shown up here with papers from the Chief Priest that give him license to do the same to us."

But the Master said, "Don't argue. Go! I have picked him as my personal representative to non-Jews and kings and Jews. And now I'm about to show him what he's in for—the hard suffering that goes with this job." So, Ananias went and found the house, placed his hands on blind Saul, and said, "Brother Saul, the Master sent me, the same Jesus you saw on your way here. He sent me so you could see again and be filled with the Holy Spirit." No sooner were the words out of his mouth than something like scales fell from Saul's eyes—he could see again! He got to his feet, was baptized, and sat down with them to a hearty meal." Acts 9:10-19 MSG.

This was a "Donkey" job for sure! Peterson translates it well, "You can't be serious...."Don't argue. Go!" The world has never been the same since this story unfolded. We started with a "Donkey Job" turned Jesus' parade. We conclude with this little story of obedience resulting in most of the New Testament being written by Paul and his missionary work in Europe (Macedonian Call), resulting in the Gospel being carried to North and South America so most of us reading this text could know Jesus! I am saying that "Yes, Donkey Jobs" usually leads to something big in God's Kingdom. Our job? Say, "Yes, Lord."

Reflection and Discussion Questions

1. Introduction – Tell some encounter with a pre-Christian and did you feel "awkward"?

2. Have you done a 'donkey job' for your family, job? How did you feel afterwards?

3. Which of the Biblical stories of 'donkey moments' spoke to you and challenged your everyday life? Why?

4. In what ways did you experience God intervene in your 'donkey job'? Did God give a Scripture, song, peace in your soul, audible voice?

5. What challenge are you facing this week that we can pray for you?

Notes

_____
_____
_____
_____
_____
_____
_____
_____

Chapter Three
YES!

I've tried everything, and nothing helps. I'm at the end of my rope. Is there no one who can do anything for me? Romans 7:24 MSG

It was the second day, Wednesday, February 4. The day before, "I found my way to that altar and told the Lord I was sorry for my failures and sin. I was so frustrated. I had prayed similar prayers so often. Considering my heritage, it was extremely embarrassing to me. Peace in my heart soon arrived."[24] "I then began to enjoy the awesome event that was taking place. Lines formed across the platform of Hughes Auditorium, Asbury College, Wilmore, Kentucky, of students waiting to share their newfound joy in Christ. It was a joy expressed with great exuberance yet orderly. People waited patiently to describe what God had just done for them."[25]

"I had stayed up all night in Hughes Auditorium experiencing the most exciting experience I had ever had. People were giving their testimonies, asking for prayer for themselves and others, and singing praises to God at the top of their lungs. God answered those prayers right before our eyes in hours, short minutes, and sometimes seconds! It was just awesome! No matter how impossible they may have been, the prayers seemed to be answered quickly. God was on the move! We were on the move. We were all swept up in it. The floodgates of heaven were open, it was raining answered prayer as people were coming to Christ on that campus and wherever the witnesses of this God Resurrection-power-driven event could tell it. .... It was on! It felt like we were living on the pages of the New Testament. No one wanted to miss a report or miracle. It was riveting.

Finally, on Wednesday noon, I reluctantly went to the cafeteria, quickly ate, and headed to my dorm room for some sleep. It had been over 24 hours. I slept about four hrs., showered, and hurried back to

---

[24] Wright, Gary. He Just Showed Up!: An Eyewitness to Revival (p. 42). Wright Stuff Publishing. Kindle Edition.
[25] Ibid., 43.

the auditorium, wondering what I had missed. The Head Resident of my dorm was sharing his testimony as I found a seat on the right of the auditorium I entered. He was not a college student. He attended Asbury Seminary across the street. He said, "God has done something wonderful for me, filled me with his Spirit." He stated several things he already knew were new in his life and rejoiced at God's Presence in His life. Well, I was glad for him, but it somewhat stole the joy for me. I had heard all my life, because of my parents and family, the theology that a Christian needs to be "filled with the Spirit." I think I understood my dad's preaching on the subject. He said that after one accepts Christ, we have the third person of the Trinity in our life. However, does He have us? Acts 2 was recited and used to show that believers could have additional power in their lives if they would make Him Lord of their lives and not just the Savior of their sins. Give themselves entirely to God... I knew this and could state various theologies, from reformed to charismatic views. One thing I did know, this had never happened to me.

As I sat in chapel that Wednesday afternoon, I sensed the Lord saying, "Wouldn't you like to have that power of Me in you, in your life?" "Oh, yes!" I said. "But this Holy Spirit thing has never happened to me, Lord." I had been filling pulpits of country churches for preaching even before I got my driver's license. I preached my first sermon in our little country church when I was ten years old.

However, at that moment, as I set in Hughes and one of America's greatest outpourings of the Spirit, it was like God turned on a video in my mind, and I started seeing the faces of people in the churches where I had preached. I desired to be used of the Lord, but I could not think of one person who sought the Lord because of my preaching. "Wouldn't you have liked to have helped them?" I sensed Him saying. "Yes!" "Is this Him pushing me in that Spirit-filled direction?" "Does this "Anointing" as my family called it, really exist? Is there more? Is there something else He can do to me?

Is this the "Yes" or "No" dilemma? I remember thinking, "If I go to the altar, everyone will think I am a backslidden preacher." Funny, I had just gone to the altar to pray in front of everyone the day before. Why? Because I was a backslidden preacher. I decided I had nothing to lose, but my pride, and I no longer had much of that. I got up, walked to the altar, knelt, and said, "God, I do not know if anything of this "being filled with the Spirit" exists. I do not know if you can make me different, but it is me if anyone ever needs you to change them. But Lord, if this (meaning what my dad and others had preached and testified to) does not exist and I just need to try harder to please you, obey you, I will just keep trying."

I suppose it was not a great prayer of faith, but it was totally sincere. I told Him He could do anything He wanted to do with me. There was a "Yes, go ahead, please." I felt such discontent and despair about my condition and awareness that I failed Him daily. I gave myself to Him as completely as I knew how. I surrendered every hope and dream at that moment to His purposes, not mine. A few weeks later, I identified with Sammy Tippit when he said, "This time, I figuratively placed my desires in a casket. I placed my wife in that casket, my car, my few belongings, and even my secret desire to be another Billy Graham. I placed everything I could think of in that casket, and then I climbed in, telling God I was willing to die to self."[26][63] I now reached up and pulled the casket lid down, and that Gary Wright died. I was desperate. All around me the glory of the Lord was being experienced. It was a Committed Beyond Choice moment. "Yes!" to Him, "No1" to anything else. Maybe, just maybe, there was something more.

Moses explained his moment like this, "At once, Moses fell to the ground and worshiped, saying, "Please, O Master, if you see anything good in me, please Master, travel with us, hard-headed as these people are. Forgive our iniquity and sin. Own us, possess us." (Exodus 34:8-9 MSG). Those last four words, "own us (me), possess us (me)" are still my prayer fifty-three years later. "Please, Lord, if you don't go with me, let's call off this trip." He took the words right out of my heart! In my heart and spirit, I sensed a "Yes!" coming. I sensed that God had heard me and that He was sending "something more" my way. I felt like a catcher who was waiting for the ball after the pitcher had thrown it. Heaven, God, was sending something my way!

---

[26] Tippiy/

Suddenly, a shot of overwhelming joy went through my innermost being. I jumped to my feet and shouted a yell of joyous victory. I did not mean to shout; it just came out. A senior from my dorm had knelt next to me to pray with me. He said, "Ought, Oh! We have a shouting Quaker!" I felt like an overflowing fountain, a mixture of joy, peace, and empowering strength. I hugged a few people, walked back to a middle aisle seat, and sat down. Walking, I kept thinking that what I felt inside was familiar. "Where have I experienced this before? I have felt this before?" And then, like a tsunami wave, it registered, "This "new" I felt inside of me was what I had felt around my daddy all my life." He had the present tense of Jesus, the Holy Spirit in and with him. He had the Presence! The Presence of Jesus! And now, I knew it was in me! Me!

Oh, anyone else could have such, but not failure ridden me!" I wept openly for joy. I weep now as I type. I am so unworthy that He would put Himself in me…. But He did, He has, and undeservingly, it is still there! He had come to live in me in a way I had never experienced before. Paul described it this way in Galatians 2:20 NIV: "I have been crucified with Christ; it is no longer I who live, but Christ lives in me; and the life which I now live in the flesh, I live by faith in the Son of God, who loved me and gave Himself for me."[27] I have never been the same. He did do "something more" in me. I said "Yes," to His way as much as I knew and "No," to the non-Jesus stuff and asked Him to change me. He did.

So, Gary Wright lived happily ever after and stayed away from the struggle of sin and shame. Yea, right! I wish. As I write today, the Asbury Revival 1970 moment was 53 years and two days ago. Again! Something indescribable happened to me that day. I did not know that day; it would just get better. I did not realize the closeness with Jesus, the intimacy with Him, and the conversations would continue to increase. I did not know that from that day on when I stood before people, He would be with me in a way that would also change other people's lives. No, the joyful, overwhelming energy is not felt like it was that day all day, but it is still there. I wore a new brand. He "owed

---

[27] Wright, Gary. He Just Showed Up!: An Eyewitness to Revival (pp. 45-48). Wright Stuff Publishing. Kindle Edition.

me" He "possessed me." I was not mine; I was His. He branded my heart. I still struggle, fifty-three years later, to label what happened to me in theological terminology. Something deep changed.

Growing up in the Holiness movement, it seemed to be a destination achievement, labeled, cataloged, and celebrated, then put away so one could say, "I got it!" If what happened to me was an "Acts 2" type of experience, it was a beginning, not a final destination. It is a Christ follower establishing Lordship and ownership and being possessed by the Master. This, in turn, allows the Spirit of Jesus, the Holy Spirit, to give Himself in the same way the recipients in Acts 2 needed. The Book of Acts isn't the end of the New Testament or the church. It is the beginning of the church and life as we know it today!

"With the arrival of Jesus, the Messiah, that fateful dilemma is resolved. Those who enter into Christ's being-here-for-us no longer have to live under a continuous, low-lying black cloud. A new power is in operation. The Spirit of life in Christ, like a strong wind, has magnificently cleared the air, freeing you from a fated lifetime of brutal tyranny at the hands of sin and death. God went for the jugular when he sent his own Son. He didn't deal with the problem as something remote and unimportant. In his Son, Jesus, he personally took on the human condition, entered the disordered mess of struggling humanity in order to set it right once and for all. The law code, weakened as it always was by fractured human nature, could never have done that."[28]

I believe we are given the Holy Spirit at our salvation. He is all the Gospel of John describes the Comforter *(Paraclete)* to be and more. However, I have observed that the Father God did not have all of me in the deepest way. Is it possible that this life-changing experience is so Holy, so intimate, it is too great for words? Is it possible that each generation struggles with the vocabulary because the previous generation's vocabulary cannot express this awesome, continuing, intimate experience with the Him of the present?

I would testify to many other spiritual discontents' "death of self" moments since then. "Yes," to the Refiner's fire. Thank the Lord, I

---

[28] Romans 8:1-4 MSG

was an eighteen-year-old, immature boy trying to become a man. Most of these "Yes," again, moments did not come with the same emotional impact. Some did.

Nevertheless, they were important to expose my need for Him and less of me. The living Christ in me is continually working to make me more like my Heavenly Father. Yet, it is me He is living in, and empowering to do His work. I used to think it was so He could use me to complete His mission. There is that. But it is more than that. He wants me to be his boy, son, and child and experience the unique experience of the Father/ Son relationship, "Oneness." There are days I forget, and I do not act like He is my Father, but as my earthly father taught me, He is not giving up on me.

George Barna says, "The holiness journey is a white-knuckles adventure on earth. At the end of the ride there may be peace, serenity, love, and joy, but along the way there will be tension, disappointment, conflict, uncertainty and more. All of those emotions and experiences may be put in our path to challenge us to grow. Naturally, there will be temptations and trials thrown at you by the enemy, but we ought not to give that adversary too much credit. God is in charge. He may allow various temptations to confront you, but it is always with a divine purpose in mind."[29]

So, what is the solution? What did the Apostle Paul mean when he wrote, "For the Son of God, Christ Jesus (the Messiah), Who has been preached among you by us, by myself, Silvanus, and Timothy, was not Yes and No; but in Him, it is [always the divine] Yes. For as many as are the promises of God, they all find their Yes [answer] in Him [Christ]. For this reason, we also utter the Amen (Yes, so be it) to God through Him [in His Person and by His agency] to the glory of God."[30]

"Those who think they can do it on their own end up obsessed with measuring their own moral muscle but never get around to exercising it in real life. Those who trust God's action in them find that God's Spirit is in them—living and breathing God!" But if God himself has taken up residence in your life, you can hardly be thinking more of

---

[29] Barna, George.
[30] 2 Corinthians 1:19-20 AMPC

yourself than of Him. Anyone, of course, who has not welcomed this invisible but clearly present God, the Spirit of Christ, won't know what we're talking about."[31]

I stood on stage an invited a young man to the stage. Holding a $5 bill I asked, "Who do you think this belongs to?" "You," he replied. "That is right," I said, "my wife let me have it before I came." "Since it is mine and I own it," I continued, "I can spend it any way I choose. I looked at the young man and said, "Do you know how I want to spend it?" Shaking his head, he said, "No." "I want to give it to you." I handed it to the young man. "It's yours. You own it now. It's no longer mine. Because you own it you can spend it anywhere, any way you choose." As the young man returned to his seat, I reminded him, "It pays to go to church."

I then looked at the audience and said, "Isn't this what God is asking? Like the dollar bill, He gives us life. We have "free will." We have choices and can spend that one life He gave us in any way we choose. However, He asks us to give our lives back to Him to spend anywhere, anyway, any purpose He chooses." I lay another dollar bill on the altar saying, " Is there anyone here who would publicly say to the Lord, " Here is my

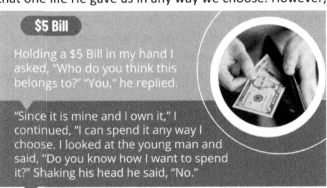

$5 Bill

Holding a $5 Bill in my hand I asked, "Who do you think this belongs to?" "You," he replied.

"Since it is mine and I own it," I continued, "I can spend it any way I choose. I looked at the young man and said, "Do you know how I want to spend it?" Shaking his head he said, "No."

"I want to give it to you." I handed it to the young man. "It's yours. You own it now. It's no longer mine. Because you own it you can spend it anywhere, any way you choose."

"Isn't this what God is asking? Like the $5 Bill He gives us life. We have "free will." We have choices and can spend that one life He gave us anyway we choose. However, He asks us to give our lives back to Him to spend anywhere, anyway, any purpose He chooses."

---

[31] Romans 8:5,9 MSG.

life, spend my life however you choose. I don't own my life anymore. You own it now."

Okay, Jesus, Perfect Jesus, is the "Divine Yes," but what does that look like in people who are Christians, Christ-following humans, who are far from perfect? If I become a Spirit-filled Christian and I still face "Yes and "No" dilemmas, what does obedience, "Yes," look like?

Reflection and Discussion Questions

1. What is the most important truth described in this chapter? Why is it important?
2. . Tell a short story of the best God's powerful service you have been involved in. What made it seem so to you? What was the immediate result? What was the longer lasting result in your life?
3. Revivals and outpourings of the Holy Spirit in North America have mostly taken place on college and university campuses then spread to local churches. Why do you think this pattern exists?
4. What tools have you learned to help you win the battle of your heart with the Lord? Who is Lord in your life, your agenda, or God's agenda?
5. What were the patterns of revival described by the author in this chapter? How can that help us in our community?
6. What does 2 Cor 12:1-19-20 mean to you in your everyday life? Give examples.
7. What prerequisites does the author describe as steps to being filled with the Holy Spirit?
8. Discuss His Lordship and ownership of your life. What does it look like when God owns us?

Notes

Chapter Four
Eight Seconds of Shame

Then Jesus stood up again and said to the woman, "Where are your accusers? Didn't even one of them condemn you?" "No, Lord," she said. And Jesus said, "Neither do I. Go and sin no more."

John 8: 10-11 NLT

Why do I fail the Lord when I try so hard to live a committed life to and for Christ? My most spiritual severe flops have been after I wanted to be a *Committed Beyond Choice* Christ follower. This journey to change, and transform into Christlikeness, is a hard-fought and scary road. Yet, it is the most fulfilling experience we can have in life. At the end of his life, not as a young Christian, Paul said, " I want to know Christ and experience the mighty power that raised him from the dead. I want to suffer with him, sharing in his death."[32] Reading the Bible and understanding its characters encourage me on this ever-challenging Jesus walk.

That Sunday evening, the disciples met behind locked doors because they feared the Jewish leaders. Suddenly, Jesus was standing there among them! "Peace be with you," he said. He showed them the wounds in his hands and his side as he spoke. They were filled with joy when they saw the Lord! Again, he said, "Peace be with you. As the Father has sent me, so I am sending you." Then he breathed on them and said, "Receive the Holy Spirit. If you forgive anyone's sins, they are forgiven. If you do not forgive them, they are not forgiven."

"One of the twelve disciples, Thomas (nicknamed the Twin),[c] was not with the others when Jesus came. They told him, "We have seen the Lord!" But he replied, "I won't believe it unless I see the nail wounds in his hands, put my fingers into them, and place my hand into the wound in his side." John 20 NLT

Have you ever said to yourself, "Why in the world did I say that? Or what was I thinking? Or why did I do that?" Most of the time, those

---

[32] Philippians 310 NLT

don't turn into significant issues. But sometimes, just a few words turn into an ugly monster.

That happened to one person in the Bible. It only took him eight seconds to say it in English. I call it "Eight seconds of shame." He was one of Jesus' guys. He was on the ministry team and one of "The 12." His name was Thomas. Jesus died on the cross. That's the setting. Jesus died on the cross, He had resurrected, and now He's in those forty days between the Resurrection and Ascension. Those 40 days, if you study them, are all about Jesus going from person to person and their self-inflicted injuries, usually because of their relation to Him, and He's healing them and fixing them. What he did in those 40 days was incredible, all of which had to do with those like us who need fixing from our self-inflicted injuries.

I don't know about you; even though I grew up going to church, I seldom heard messages or lessons of any kind about Thomas. And yet I find him to be such a compelling story. John 20 records Jesus appearing to what was left of his team. Sunday night after the resurrection, there are just ten of the disciples. Thomas isn't there. It says. "One of the twelve disciples, Thomas, nicknamed the twin." He obviously had a twin brother and was not with the others when Jesus came. And they went, and they told Thomas, "We have seen the Lord, but he replied, and here are his eight seconds of shame, "I won't believe it unless I see the nail wounds in his hands. And put my fingers into them and place my hand into the wound in his side." He wasn't in the small group that Sunday night. He was missing. We probably all missed a small group one night or another, right? And we have all kinds of reasons we miss small groups. I have to ask, what was this about? What caused this response? I don't believe what you just said. He said to the other ten. Judas was gone, so there were just eleven in the small group now. And they were meeting behind locked doors and because they were scared what happened to Jesus would happen to them. And so, they locked all the doors. And then, "Bing III" (I don't know what sound effect to use.) Jesus suddenly appeared. And his first words were? "Peace" or "Shalom." "Shalom" is that multilayered, wonderful Hebrew word. "Peace be with you." He's trying to calm their nerves. I don't know if they all jumped when he suddenly appeared. I don't know. Jesus is there. How does He get in here? He didn't use the door.

They all report all this to Thomas. "We've seen Him, and He's alive!" Thomas said, "I don't believe that." What's that all about?

Did you know there are only three passages that talk about Thomas? Notice that after Thomas died, after the Bible was written, we added an adjective on the front of his name when we talked about him. We do this all because of those eight seconds. And we call him not just the Apostle Thomas. We don't call him just Thomas. We call him "Doubting Thomas." Just eight seconds! Now, they didn't call him that while he was still alive. Since he died, we started calling him this "doubting" Thomas. Eight seconds and we treat him like this?

Now we live in a social media world where one can be videoed and have eight seconds that bring shame, even if it doesn't represent how you live. Cancel culture. I feel like it's unfair what we do to this guy. Calling him "Doubting Thomas" when I think the story shows other reasons for his actions besides a lack of faith. Here are the three times we meet him in Scripture: 1) Jesus and his twelve ministry team would hang out in a town called Bethany. They hung out at a house owned by a guy named Lazarus and his two sisters, Mary and Martha. Jesus and his team never slept one night in Jerusalem that we know of. They would always go to this little village where you can almost see the Temple Dome. Bethany, that's where they would stay. Lazarus apparently had a big enough house. Jesus had a big ministry team. It was not just Jesus and the Twelve but included others like the women who cooked and provided for the group. Obviously, they had a close relationship with Jesus.

Jesus is teaching up in Galilee to the northside, in what we call the Evangelistic or Gospel Triangle. And he'd go from village to village.[33] (Map Image of Gospel Triangle[34]) This is where most Jesus chose to make his home.

---

[33] The Evangelistic or Gospel Triangle is a small area between 3 cities, Capernaum, Korazm and Bethsaida. These cities form geographically a triangle. Jesus chose to make his home in Capernaum, on the northwest shores of the Sea of Galilee. The road called "Way of the Sea" ran through Capernaum.
[34] https://www.wordofgodtoday.com/evangelical-triangle/

of Jesus' ministry occurred (Approximately 80%[35]). All of the twelve disciples came from this area except possibly Judas, "Men of Galilee." Jesus is up there, and He's teaching, and he's healing, and he's preaching, and he gets word. "Your friend, your dear friend Lazarus, is deathly sick. Please come." It says in John 11, "A man named Lazarus was sick. He lived in Bethany. So the two sisters sent a

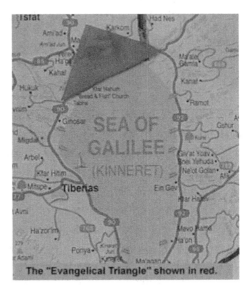

The "Evangelical Triangle" shown in red.

message to Jesus telling him, Lord, your dear friend, is very sick. His response was not what we'd expect. Jesus hung around the Evangelistic Triangle for two more days before going to Bethany. And then, when it was raised that they might go back to Bethany because Lazarus was sick, the Disciples didn't want to go. Why? Here's why, "Rabbi," they said, "Only a few days ago, the people in Judea were trying to stone you. Are we really going to go there again?" Now, I get it. That makes sense. "Are you sure we have to go back there and risk our lives?" "No!" they were saying, "Our vote is, "No!" But after two days, Jesus said, "Let's go." And they all look at each other. "I guess we're going to do this."

And that's where we have Thomas speak up. He says to other disciples. "Let's go too and die with Jesus." Now there are all kinds of personalities and mindsets today, and there were all kinds of in the twelve disciples. Obviously, if you study him, this guy is a bit of a pessimist. He's the guy on the plane when you hit some kind of disturbance, and the pilot comes on and warns you, "OK, we got disturbance coming." When the plane begins to rattle and shake, he's the one that stands up and screams, "We're all going to die!"

---

[35] http://www.jamesjanzen.com/blog/geography-101-the-triangle-of-jesus-ministry

Nevertheless, he was so committed to Jesus. He had made a choice. He believes Jesus is the Messiah, the Christ. When you study this guy, and you study these three places in scripture where it gives a description of him, he really meant, "I'm ready to die for Jesus; I'm ready to die with him."

Now Thomas had a bit different idea of who Jesus was. He thought Jesus was going to be a Messiah who would free Israel from the oppression of the Roman Empire. Most followers of Jesus shared this view. They all thought Jesus was going to be a political liberator. That Jesus Thomas was willing to die for. And so, he says to the rest, "Hey. If we go to Bethany, we know what awaits us there. My vote is let's go and die with Jesus." He was committed to that Jesus.

John 14 gives us such a precious passage that we use when we lose someone close to us. Jesus' words, "I'm going to prepare a place for you. You will always be with me where I am, and you know the way to where I'm going." I don't know about you, but when Jesus said, "I'm gonna go prepare a place for you." I'm thinking of heaven, and I'm thinking, awesome! But some of us have had that child in our family, and when you say "road trip," a whole predictable verbal discussion begins. That child asks, "How many hours is this going to take? Which way are we going? How many places are we going to stop? Are we going to stop here?" In our family, that person is now a PhD. And the question really was, "How many books do I need to take?" He asked really detailed questions, and if we didn't answer to his satisfaction, he wasn't going. But he knew he was going and really was willing to go, but he just constantly came up with a barrage of questions. "Are we there yet? And how much longer is this going to take?" Did you raise that child? We did. Thomas, he's the one who, when Jesus said, "I go to prepare a place, you know where I am going," said, "No, we don't. We don't know where you are going. Lord, we have no idea where you're going. So how can we know the way?" Is this guy Interesting? He's willing to go die. But man, he wants to know the details. Jesus took this time to answer. "I am the way the truth and the life. No one can come to the Father except through me." Jesus said, "If you want to go to heaven, I am the Interstate. I am the road you take. I am the route." He also said, "You can't get there any other way except through me." We probably all need to be reminded in this pluralistic world that we live in, where people say all religions and gods lead to the same place. Jesus said, "I, exclusively. I am the only way to heaven." According to Jesus, that truth. That is what we believe. That is the second passage where we meet Thomas.

The next and final biblical passage is where we started. Jesus resurrected. The 40-day clock is moving towards His leaving, the Ascension. The ten Apostles are behind locked doors. Thomas did not show up for Sunday night's small group. Where was he? When you look at his personality type, His commitment to the political liberation Messiah, we could have said, "he's off pouting." Why is he pouting? He's confused and deeply disappointed. The Jesus he was willing to die for was beaten, mocked, and executed. Jesus was not who he thought he was. He is devastated. He did not show up for the Sunday night small group.

You can believe in Jesus and be willing to die for him, yet you can still make a mess of things. It only takes eight seconds for Thomas to make the mistake we do not seem willing to forgive him for, "Doubting Thomas." Just eight seconds of shame. Thomas did not show up in small group, but someone did. Thomas wasn't there! He missed Jesus!

I love it; the small group reaches out to him. They return to him and say, "Hey dude, you missed it. Jesus showed up at small group. You weren't there." "I don't believe you." I believe that one reason he didn't believe it is... he didn't want to. He didn't want to believe Jesus was different from his preferred God concept. Jesus was asking him to live on earth without his physical presence. I don't think Thomas wanted to do that. He wanted to live in the physical presence of Jesus or die for that liberator Jesus. At this point, I don't think he wanted to live at all.

My daddy used to say the problem with "living sacrifices," as they are called for in Romans 12, is that when you lay a living sacrifice down on the altar, it tends to crawl off and go away to our own choices. Do you see what Jesus was asking Thomas to do? "I want you to make this transition. I'm not going to hang around physically. I want you to live for me. After I physically leave this earth, Thomas, live what I demonstrated and taught you." That's not the Jesus Thomas wanted.

I can't help but think of the missionary James Calvert. When James Calvert went out as a missionary to the cannibals of the Fiji islands, the ship captain tried to turn him back, saying, "You'll lose your life and the lives of those with you if you go among those savages." Calvert replied, "We died before we came here."[36] "It's too late. They can't kill us. We already died before we came here." That means, " I'm saying yes to Jesus." No matter what I am faced with, God is asking me to do this. I've decided ahead of time. I've made the commitment. My answer is, "Yes, Jesus, I'll go where you want me to go. I'll do what you want me to do."

And yet, as we do that every day, we face things and think, "I don't think I want to do that. I don't think I want to go there." Then we got to thinking, but I told him I would. I didn't know what to say yes to, but I told him I would.

I love the fact that God, Jesus, didn't give up on Thomas. Eight days later, Small group. This time, Thomas shows up! Guess who else showed up. Jesus appears. He speaks "peace" to them again. The doors were locked. Suddenly, as before, Jesus stood among them, "Peace be with you." Notice what he does exactly next. Immediately Jesus turns to Thomas and says, "Put your finger here and look at my hands and feet. Put your hand into the wound in my side from the spear. Don't be faithless any longer, believe." I want you to notice that God doesn't quit on us when we mess up and have our eight seconds of shame. Jesus doesn't quit on us. The Holy Spirit does not quite on us. The heavenly Trinity is for us, "Who can be against us?"

He pursues those injured because of their relationship with Him during those forty days after his resurrection and up to his ascension. He appears to Simon Peter and says, "Hey, let's have breakfast. You betrayed me three times. I'm not concerned about that. I'm just concerned about you being healed." Mary Magdalene, all kinds of self-inflicted wounds. Demons. But at the tomb, Jesus said, "Mary." She

---

[36] Foreman, Emily. We Died Before We Came Here: A True Story of Sacrifice and Hope . The Navigators. Kindle Edition.

said, "Master! He was really saying the same thing to her as He was saying to Thomas. "Don't cling to me, babe. We have got to change the world, and I will use you. Don't cling to what we've had in the past because I have greater things for us."

I think the first person he appeared to was that brother of his, that half-brother of his, James[37], who would, I'm sure, was the one who said, "Jesus, You need to leave, take your salvation roadshow somewhere else. Because you're embarrassing our family." That brother was one of the first people He appeared to in those 40 days. History says that James was so guilt ridden, he refused to eat or drink." I'm not going to drink until I've seen the Master." It would be a stretch to think that your brother is God. You might think your brother acts like he's God, but to actually believe he is, that's got to be a stretch.

I want you to know that Jesus refused to leave earth without healing these self-inflicted wounded people that he loves so dearly, and one of them was Thomas. The great Italian artist Caravaggio painted a picture of the healing moment. In the painting, Jesus is holding Thomas's hand and placing his finger in his wound. I mean, that's what Thomas said, "I won't believe until I have touched His wounds." And Jesus, according to the Bible, says, "Reach, reach out here and touch me. Put your hand in my wound. Go ahead." In the painting, Thomas can't even look at Jesus. Have you had that moment when you couldn't even look at him? I did something or said something so stupid, so bad, I couldn't even look at Him. Have you been there? You may ask, "How do you know about that?" Because I've been there so many times. "Lord, don't even look at me. I can't believe I said it. Can't believe it did it." I think the artist Caravaggio got it right.

Then Jesus told him, "You believe because you've seen me. Blessed are those who believe without seeing me. But the secret? The secret to being healed? It was not just reaching out and touching Jesus; it was what Thomas said. He may have had eight seconds of verbal

---

[37] The Catholic church believes the New Test reference to Jesus' brothers were actualy cousins as Mary remained a virgin for life. The Eastern Ortodox believe Mary remained a virgin for life but that Joseph was a widower with children from a previous marriage when he married Marry. The Protestant few is that Mary and Joseph had children after the miraculous virgin birth of Jesus.

shame. But here's what he said, "My Lord. And my God. My Lord. Oh my God." And when he used the word "Lord," this is what that word meant. "You are my Lord. You own me. You own me. From this day forward, you own me. I'll go where you want me to go. My answer to your question is "YES!". What is E. Stanley Jones called the "Divine Yes," I will go. I will. I've already decided "Yes" to whatever you ask me to do.

You know what? Jesus is still asking. People like you and me. Reach out to me. Touch me. Can you almost hear him ask? "I dare you. If you do it, you won't ever be the same."

Do you know what my response is? I was four years old when I gave my heart to Christ. Now you say, "How could you know what you were doing when you were four years old?" If you were raised in the family, I was raised in at 4, you know. So, I've served Jesus now for 68 years. I'm 72. But here's my prayer still today. "Jesus, please don't leave me this way. Please." As I draw close 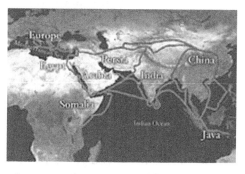 to him. Each day, I realize things about me that are not like Him. I want to be like Him. But I can't be like Him unless I'm with him and he touches me. I have learned if I show up to be with Him, He constantly shows up to be with me. No, I don't sense His Presence in the same exuberance of the 185 hours of the Asbury Revival. Yet, when He comes, it is built on all these years of His faithfulness and love. It is more than enough; it is more than I could imagine. Like he says to Thomas, "You make the decision, reach out and touch me, my wounds, my nail scars, the wound in my side. If you do that, you will never be the same. I will send you as a messenger of the gospel to your neighbors. to the world." Now what was the result?

Casting Crowns Song: East to West

https://youtu.be/1BqS6BBDpM8

Here I am, Lord, and I'm drowning in Your sea of forgetfulness.

The chains of yesterday surround me, I yearn for peace and rest.

I don't want to end up where You found me.

And it echoes in my mind, keeps me awake tonight.

I know You've cast my sin as far as the east is from the west.

And I stand before You now as, as though I've never sinned.

But today I feel like I'm just one mistake away from You leavin' me this way.

Jesus, can You show me just how far the east is from the west?

'Cause I can't bear to see the man I've been come risin' up in me again.

In the arms of Your mercy, I find rest

'Cause You know just how far the east is from the west.

From one scarred hand to the other.[38]

The Bible doesn't tell us, but history does. I got a map for you. Look at this map.[39] If you go down to the bottom of India, there on the right, you see those red lines to the southeast bottom of India. That's where Thomas went. History records it. And then he went up the East Coast there. In fact, World Renewal has a ministry partner in a city called Chennai. And right outside of Chennai is St. Thomas Mount. They say that is where Thomas is buried. He may have traveled further mile-wise than any of the other apostles, possibly rivaling the Apostle Paul. "Committed Beyond Choice Thomas" planted churches all over India. He is the only apostle that planted churches where they still use his name and have from the beginning. They call themselves "St. Thomas Christians," the Great Mar Thoma Church of India.[40] "The name Thomas remains quite popular among the Saint Thomas Christians of the Indian

---

[38] Song by Casting Crowns. East to West.
[39] https://en.wikipedia.org/wiki/Thomas_the_Apostle.
[40] The origins of the Mar Thoma Church go back to the work of the Apostle St Thomas in the south-west region of India. According to the tradition Saint Thomas came to India in 52 AD and founded the church there.

subcontinent. Besides India, many churches in the Middle East and southern Asia also mention Apostle Thomas in their historical traditions as the first evangelist to establish those churches, the Assyrian Church of the East, the early church of Sri Lanka."[41] It is there historians say Thomas laid down his life. Jesus said, "Touch the place of the spear." Ironically, Thomas was speared and gave his life after planting churches all over India, history says. How can we call him the doubter?[42]

I am positive that the adjective "Doubting" does not precede his name in heaven. Eight seconds of shame turn into a fruitful, magnificent, and extraordinary life. Obviously, his healing came out of that moment. Jesus said, "Hey, come here. Touch me." The man, so full of shame, reached out. He touched Jesus, and Jesus touched him back, and "by his wounds we are healed." How about it dear friend? Do you need Jesus' healing touch? Do you have an "eight seconds of shame" moment? Are you like me, even after all these years? "Lord, please don't leave me this way."

Reflection and Discussion Questions

1. What are some of Thomas's admirable traits?

2. What actions show the other disciples had not given up on Thomas?

3. Describe and define some public people examples of "culture canceling" today.

3. Describe a time when other people refused to give up on you?

4. Have you ever felt you had failed so much that you were "one step away from Him leaving me this way?"

5. What do you notice or observe about Jesus' restoration approach to Thomas?

---

[41] https://en.wikipedia.org/wiki/Thomas_the_Apostle.

[42] It should be said that not all church historians accept this author's acceptance of Thomas's role in India. I encourage you to study and form your own view of church history.

6. Could you describe a similar experience of Christ healing you of your "Eight Seconds of Shame?"

7. Close in praying for your group and again for your 3rd chair loved ones.

Notes

_____

_____

_____

_____

_____

_____

_____

_____

_____

_____

Chapter Five
From One Generation to Another

Write these commandments that I've given you today on your
hearts. Get them inside of you and then get them inside your children.
Talk about them wherever you are, sitting at home or walking in the
street; talk about them from the time you get up in the morning to when
you fall into bed at night.
Tie them on your hands and foreheads as a reminder; inscribe them on
the doorposts of your homes and on your city gates.

Deuteronomy 6:6-9 MSG

I think I know something about you if you have children. You would give your very life for your children and grandchildren. They are the love of our lives, correct? We want our children and grandchild to know Jesus, to experience Jesus. We would gladly lay down our lives so they would know the Lord Jesus, experience life with Him on earth, and know they are headed to heaven. However, God asks us to give our lives as a living sacrifice before those in our lives. The Apostle Paul states that we Christ-followers are called to be quoted:

"Therefore, I urge you, brothers and sisters, by the mercies of God, to present your bodies [dedicating all of yourselves, set apart] as a living sacrifice, holy and well-pleasing to God, which is your rational (logical, intelligent) act of worship. 2 And do not be conformed to this world [any longer with its superficial values and customs], but be [c]transformed and progressively changed [as you mature spiritually] by the renewing of your mind [focusing on godly values and ethical attitudes], so that you may prove [for yourselves] what the will of God is, that which is good and acceptable and perfect [in His plan and purpose for you]." Romans 12:1-2. Amplified

Paul says we need to live as a "Living Sacrifice" to the Lord Jesus. My dad used to say, "The problem of the "Living Sacrifice is that a live sacrifice can easily crawl off the altar." Eugene Peterson translated

"Living sacrifice" as: "Take your everyday, ordinary life—your sleeping, eating, going-to-work, and walking-around life—and place it before God as an offering."

Moses wrote, "I lavish unfailing love ("Hesed," "When the person from whom I have a right to expect nothing gives me everything.")to a thousand generations. I forgive iniquity, rebellion, and sin. But I do not excuse the guilty. I lay the sins of the parents upon their children and grandchildren; the entire family is affected— even children in the third and fourth generations." Exodus 34:7 NLT

What does this "Living Sacrifice" look like? Let's look to a biblical story to understand what this "Living Sacrifice looks like. Is this "Committed Beyond Choice," "Yes!" living or behavior?

Story of Joshua's Last Words -Final Instructions "Death Bed Confession."

"Then Joshua summoned all the tribes of Israel … So, they came .. This is what the Lord, the God of Israel, says: With your very own eyes you saw what I did." (Miracles: Manna, Water, Cloud-GPS) "The people of Israel served the Lord throughout the lifetime of Joshua and of the elders who outlived him—those who had personally experienced all that the Lord had done for Israel." The people of Israel said, "He (The Lord) performed mighty miracles before our very eyes." Joshua 24 NLT

God is speaking to two generations of Israel, reminding them of His miracles they have seen with their own eyes. They confess that they have seen and experienced His miracles.

"And the Israelites served the Lord throughout the lifetime of Joshua and the leaders who outlived him—those who had seen all the great things the Lord had done for Israel... "That entire generation passed away; a new generation grew up that had not personally experienced the Lord's Presence or seen what he had done for Israel." Judges 2 NET

The Judges passage describes the previous two generations starting with Joshua's generation, then describes a third generation, the generation of Joshua's grandchildren. Unbelievably, they are entirely without God. How can the grandchildren of Joshua's great "Committed

Beyond Choice type" generation "neither know the Lord nor what He had done for Israel?" How can that happen? Is this our problem today? Has the enemy of God stolen our children and grandchildren?

According to researcher George Barna, those who claim to be "Born Again" Christians in the United States of America do not use the Bible to be their moral compass. "Let's put this in perspective. As of 2003, the United States has about 210 million adults. About 175 million of them claim to be Christian. About 80 million are born-again Christians. Roughly 7 million have a biblical worldview. That is just one out of every 30 adults in this nation." Well, what did Barna use to measure America's biblical worldview?

"For years, we have used a standard battery of six questions that reveal people's adoption of central biblical principles. Specifically, we examine the following beliefs:

• God is the all-knowing, all-powerful Creator of the universe who still rules that universe today.

• When Jesus Christ was on earth, He lived a sinless life.

• Satan is not just a symbol of evil but is an actual, living entity.

• A person cannot earn his or her eternal salvation by being good or doing good things for other people; that salvation is the free gift of God.

• Every person who believes in Jesus Christ has a personal responsibility to share his or her faith in Him with other people who believe differently.

• The Bible is totally accurate in all that it teaches. These six statements are, of course, an incomplete inventory of a person's belief system."

Barna says 98% of our U.S.A. teenagers do not believe the above six statements. To be totally honest, I am stunned at these findings.

Other research points to the same conclusions. The Pew Research Center, September 10, 2020, says, "Research has suggested that much of the movement away from religion among young adults occurs after they come of age, move out of their childhood homes, or otherwise gain a measure of independence from their parents. This pattern fits a psychological model of religious and spiritual development, pointing to a post-adolescent trend toward autonomy. In early adulthood, there seems to be a considerable decline in the public aspects of religion – such as religious service participation –. In contrast, more private aspects of religion, such as prayer and the personal importance of religion, decline more moderately."

"Some findings from the new survey are consistent with this pattern. For one, many teens say their participation in religious activities occurs mainly because of their parent's desires, not their own. And even though teens may attend religious worship services as often as their parents, they are less likely to say religion is important in their lives. Moreover, consistent with previous research, the survey shows that religious attendance declines in the final two years of high school."

Israel had a problem; we have a problem.

Three Chairs that Represent these three generations: Let's picture these three generations Joshua and Judges describe the object of three chairs. First Chair is Joshua's Generation, labeled the "Company of the Committed." The first Chair is Joshua's generation. They are the generation who lead Israel out of Egypt. They experienced God saving them from Pharoah's army of war chariots at the Red Sea. They saw and experienced God's miracles, the mana from heaven, water out of a rock, and the cloud of Fire in the sky, which was their GPS to lead them in the wilderness. They are people of faith. They had the miracle-working Presence of God in their lives, led by Moses and Joshua. Our founding pastors and elders of our churches are usually examples of this kind of First Chair, "Company of the Committed" Romans 12, and "Living Sacrifice."

Third Chair generation is those whose parents are believers of God, yet they were a generation who "grew up that had not personally experienced the Lord's presence or seen what he had done for Israel." I would call them the Company of the Confused. Why were they lost and confused? They had such godly grandparents. What happened?

64

The Generation of the Second Chair had also, along with their parents, seen all God had done, and experienced His miracles and Presence. Nevertheless, they became the Company of those who Compromised. As they traveled and settled in their Promised by God land, they looked at those people of other groups around them and wanted what they had. By the end of Judges, this statement reflects the results: "People did whatever they felt like doing." Judges 21:25 MSG In other words, there was no biblical worldview from the teachings God had given through Moses and those teachers of the Law. I believe, like Israel, there has been a gradual erosion of the use of the Bible and its teachings to guide our moral living and decisions in these generations. Barna states the findings, "While 7 percent of those in the Builder and Seniors generations (those in their late fifties or older) base their moral decisions on the Bible and contend that morality is absolute, and 10 percent of the Baby Boomers concur, just 3 percent of the Baby Busters and only 4 percent of the oldest quarter of the Mosaic generation have a similar perspective.[2] Not surprisingly, women are nearly twice as likely as men to base their moral decisions on the Bible and say that morality is based on absolutes (7 percent versus 4 percent, respectively). Overall, just 6 percent of American adults possess a solid foundation on which to build a biblical worldview."

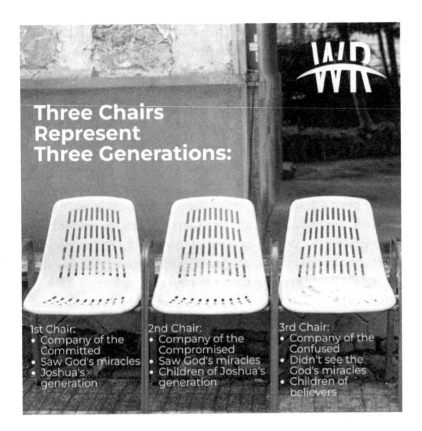

Three Chairs Represent Three Generations:

1st Chair:
- Company of the Committed
- Saw God's miracles
- Joshua's generation

2nd Chair:
- Company of the Compromised
- Saw God's miracles
- Children of Joshua's generation

3rd Chair:
- Company of the Confused
- Didn't see the God's miracles
- Children of believers

I find this appalling! Yet, I am a part of this today too. Every day we face an avalanche of non-biblical pressures that scream bigotry, intolerance, and lack of welcoming to living contrary to biblical values. I see what some have called "Family Idolatry" when parents and grandparents surrender their biblical standards and values when their family chooses to live outside of those biblical standards and values. In my lifetime, there has been an erosion of teaching the Bible to children. "In America, the first national Sunday School effort began in 1824; its purpose was to organize, evangelize and civilize. The focus was intentionally evangelical, so within the next 100 years, the Sunday School had become the primary outreach arm of the church. The Sunday School organization now expanded to include all ages. Sunday School became a way for unbelievers to be introduced to and then assimilated into the church's life. By the late 1800s, Sunday School was considered the main hope for church growth, a view that continued until the mid-twentieth century.

Sunday School attendance has slowly declined in the last 50 or so years. One factor generally agreed to be a reason for this is the shift away from evangelism and toward discipleship and fellowship over the last half-century. Studies indicate that church membership increases where Sunday Schools are thriving and growing.

The idea of Sunday School as a primary opportunity for evangelism may be new to some of us. Is it possible that a return to that model could help revitalize our churches? Has Sunday School attendance declined in your church, or is it thriving? Indeed, much has changed since the idea of a Sunday school for the reform of unruly street children was first envisioned!" Sunday School may not be an attractive model today. What is the best practice of teaching the Bible to children, youth, and adults today? What works needs to be asked? We must ask as it is being done well in many congregations.

2nd & 3rd Chair Solutions

We must have "One last shaking, from top to bottom, stem to stern. The phrase "One last shaking" means a thorough house cleaning, getting rid of all the historical and religious junk so that the unshakable essentials stand clear and uncluttered. Hebrews 12:27   The Message

What are the steps to His Presence? "You have abandoned the love you had at first. Remember therefore from where you have fallen; repent and do the work you did at first." Revelation 2: 4-5 NIV

What does that look like?

Repent-Ask Forgiveness

Remember-First Love Relationship to Jesus

Re-Do- First Steps with Jesus

Return- Cross & Path

I encourage you to follow the Trifecta of Christian Discipline: 1) Congregational Worship, 2) Small Group Bible Study, 3) Prayer and Accountability Partner

Can we afford 2nd Chair Christianity? Which Chair are we sitting in?

I sat in the church's parsonage, where I was to preach renewal and revival ministry. The pastor, who would lead the worship music that night, asked me, "What are you preaching tonight?" "Well," I call it, "Three Chairs," I said." "I don't think I have heard that one," the pastor said. His wife walked through the room, overheard the conversation, and said, "I heard it at Brown City Camp Meeting; it changed my life." The three of us looked at each other, a bit stunned. Here is her story:

"Whoever begins their fairytale life expecting the one you promised to love until death to leave you with the flimsy excuse that he doesn't want to be a husband or a father to our two precious children? This is where I found myself in 1983, with my 5-year-old & 7-year-old in tow. My sister-in-law invited us to church & after a few weeks, I gave my heart to Jesus.

Because of a poor decision to move away from where I was being disciplined, I just felt like such a loser as a woman & mother. I heard a sermon on the importance of family & the pastor stated, "Children from broken homes do not have a chance in this world." To say the least, I was devastated.

I was invited to attend Brown City Missionary Church Camp in the summer of 2002. Dr. Gary Wright was the evangelist. His sermon began with discussing the watered-down faith of 3 generations using three chairs as an illustration. Once again, my heart started to break in shame. Suddenly, the message gave this power back to God & nothing is impossible with God.

I walked away that evening with the fullness of the Holy Spirit & a new hope that Jesus saw us through. Both of my children are Jesus' Followers & they have led my grandchildren to follow Jesus. Thanks, Be To God be the glory."

Trifecta of Christian Discipline

Congreg-
ational
Worship +

Small
Group
Bible
Study +

Prayer and
Account-
ability
partner +

The night I preached at Brown City Camp, Michigan, the pastor and his wife had yet to meet. I never met her until after she had married the pastor, Hal Phillips, my roommate in college and often my preaching companion in revival services. Pastor Hal is one of my dearest friends. Our early spiritual formation in the 1970 Asbury Revival linked us for life. Since their marriage, both have excelled in ministry. Kathy became an ordained Methodist pastor. Pastor Hal will retire this month after a lifetime of extremely powerful ministry in the Methodist church. They are Committed Beyond Choice, First Chair people who have experienced the powerful blessing of God in their lives.

Reflection and Discussion Questions

1. Introduce yourself and report a 1st chair story told to you, your remarks?

2. What are some issues that 2nd chair (They knew of God's attributes, but live a life of 'comfort',

enjoy life by the battles won by 1st chair individuals)

3. What are some issues that 3rd chair (no understanding of a personal relationship with Christ)

face that a 1st or 2nd chair could handle?

4. Start a small group prayer sheet with just first names of those who are 3 rd chair who need the

Lord.

5. Spend the rest of the session in prayer for these.

Notes

Chapter Six
Restoration Breakfast

Do you love me? John 21 NLT

" Walking along the beach of Lake Galilee, Jesus saw two brothers: Simon (later called Peter) and Andrew. They were fishing, throwing their nets into the lake. It was their regular work. Jesus said to them, "Come with me. I'll make a new kind of fisherman out of you. I'll show you how to catch men and women instead of perch and bass." They didn't ask questions but immediately dropped their nets and followed. A short distance down the beach, they came upon another pair of brothers, James and John, Zebedee's sons. Sitting in a boat with their father, Zebedee, they were mending their fishnets. Jesus made the same offer to them, and they were just as quick to follow, abandoning boat and father."

` Jesus selects the leaders of His ministry team, two sets of fishing brothers. No, He did not go to the local Bible college or seminary. Jesus went to the beach. He went to the fishing dock areas of the Sea of Galilee. If you were choosing ministry team leaders, where would you start? They were not known for their Old Testament prowess. They smelled of fish and lake water. Bible scholars who have studied this bible culture contend that Zebedee & Sons Fishing Company was a very successful business. They don't say that about Peter and Andrew's family, but they could be. We know that Peter owned his own house, so there was success. But ministry to launch Christianity to an entire world? Come on now! Would you have picked these four fishermen?

On the other hand, one must admit these two sets of brothers show impressive commitment to Jesus. Three of the four would die premature deaths because of Jesus, and the fourth surviving one would suffer greatly before dying of old age. Not everyone interested in Jesus in the Gospel narratives share their (the two sets of brothers) commitment to Jesus. When complicated topics arose in Jesus' teachings (eat my flesh and drink my blood, which was forbidden to the Jews), many said. "I'm out of here!" and did not stay. They could not accept His teachings about Himself. "At this point, many of his disciples turned away and deserted him. Then Jesus turned to the Twelve and asked, "Are you also going to leave? Simon Peter replied, "Lord, to

whom would we go? You have the words that give eternal life. We believe, and we know you are the Holy One of God." Peter expresses a clear belief that Jesus is the Messiah that the Jewish nation so longed and waited for. Jesus asks His Twelve who they think He, Jesus, is, and Peter speaks for himself and the group, "Jesus and his disciples headed out for the villages around Caesarea Philippi. As they walked, he asked, "Who do the people say I am?" "Some say 'John the Baptizer,'" they said. "Others say 'Elijah.' Still, others say, 'one of the prophets.'" He then asked, "And you—what are you saying about me? Who am I?" Peter answered: "You are the Christ, the Messiah." He and the group passed the pop quiz twice! So, like most of you reading this, Peter believes Jesus is the Messiah. Unfortunately, a belief that Jesus is God does not keep us from sin. It does not protect us from sinful thoughts, actions, or words. Belief in Jesus does not put us in some perfect bubble that keeps other humans from sinning against us, causing spiritual, physical, emotional, or mental injury. Simon Peter is known for his impulsive or lack of thought-out words or actions. At the Mt. of Transfiguration, Simon Peter talks nonsense when Moses and Elijah show up to a shiny, bright, and physically glowing Jesus. "Peter exclaimed, "Rabbi, it's wonderful for us to be here! Let's make three shelters as memorials—one for you, one for Moses, and one for Elijah." He said this because he didn't really know what else to say, for they were all terrified." Most of us have had moments when caught by surprise, and we either said or did something we later found embarrassing. Peter often talked too much. Peter often acted too quickly. The Bible's credibility is raised by the transparency of its characters and players. It also encourages me that these main players are real, imperfect, and flawed humans. Jesus picked them to become His best! As my mentor, Robert Coleman would say, He selected just a few, lived with them, prepared them, then left them in charge of His church. We consider the behavior of these men as we read the Gospels it is easy to ask, "What was He, Jesus, thinking choosing these idiots?" How could He trust them to start His church?

Simon Peter's greatest error and injury was predicted, prophesied (in other words, Peter was warned) by Jesus when Simon Peter was bragging about himself. Jesus said, "It is necessary that the Son of Man proceed to an ordeal of suffering, be tried and found guilty by the elders, high priests, and religion scholars, be killed, and after three days rise up alive." He said this simply and clearly so they couldn't miss it." I believe that Simon Peter confessed the following in author John Mark's presence, "It is this way, Jesus told them, "You're all going to feel that your world is falling apart and that it's my fault. There's a Scripture that says, 'I will strike the shepherd; the sheep will scatter. "But after I am raised up, I will go ahead of you, leading the way to Galilee." Peter blurted out, "Even if everyone else is ashamed of you when things fall to pieces, I won't be." All the others said the same thing." "But Peter grabbed him in protest. Turning and seeing his disciples wavering, wondering what to believe, Jesus confronted Peter. "Peter, get out of my way! Satan, get lost! You have no idea how God works." "And Peter took Him (Peter is trying to school God) by the hand and led Him aside and then [facing Him] began to rebuke Him (Jesus)." But turning around [His back to Peter] and seeing His disciples, He rebuked Peter, saying, Get behind Me, Satan! For you do not have a mind intent on promoting what God wills, but what pleases men [you are not on God's side, but that of men]." However, my favorite description of these conversations is from Dr. Luke," "Simon, stay on your toes. Satan has tried his best to separate all of you from me, like chaff from wheat. Simon, I've prayed for you in particular that you do not give in or give out. When you have come through the time of testing, turn to your companions and give them a fresh start." Peter said, "Master, I'm ready for anything with you. I'd go to jail for you. I'd die for you!" "Jesus said, "I'm sorry to have to tell you this, Peter, but before the rooster crows you will have three times denied that you know me."

How awful! Simon tries to correct God. Have you ever done that? Yes, I have tried to school God. I have let God know that I think His timing or lack of action is way off. Nevertheless, the Good News is Jesus saying," Simon, I have prayed for you." I believe Simon Peter was being as honest as possible when he said, "Master, I am ready for anything with you." He just didn't have what it takes to follow through with it. There is then, later, that horrible moment in the Caiaphas courtyard after Peter's third denial, when Jesus' eyes turn and meet Peter's, I call it "The Look."

"At that very moment, the last word hardly off his lips, a rooster crowed. Just then, the Master turned and looked at Peter. Peter remembered what the Master said: "Before the rooster crows, you will deny me three times." He went out and cried and cried and cried." It's such an awful moment. I have been there. How could I have been so weak? I let God down. I let myself and those I love down. It's horrible, and the self-inflicted injuries are so harmful! We relive them in our minds and hearts over and over. Satan, the "accuser," loves these self-inflicted injuries. Yes, "he went out and cried and cried." Me too.

Even after the resurrection of Jesus, Jesus appears to the disciples. It is obvious Peter is still severely injured from his self-inflicted injury. Even though his wild sword swinging, courageous effort at Jesus' arrest was wrong. "Just then, Simon Peter, who was carrying a sword, pulled it from its sheath and struck the Chief Priest's servant, cutting off his right ear. Malchus was the servant's name. Jesus ordered Peter, "Put back your sword. Do you think for a minute I'm not going to drink this cup the Father gave me?" Jesus not only corrected him, then and there, in front of everyone, Jesus had to literally clean up his bloody mess by sticking poor Malchus's ear back on his head! It is interesting to me that the other Gospel writers do not name who the sword swinger was by name, but Peter's dear friend and cousin John writing about sixty years after the event, does name Peter. Integrity and respect for each other are seen in scripture and are wonderful.

John also shows the severity and confusion of Peter, and he alone records the "Let's go fishing" event of the "At least that's something I know and understand" attitude. "Simon Peter announced, "I'm going fishing." The rest of them replied, "We're going with you." They went out and got in the boat. They caught nothing that night. That had to be depressing. Sometimes, nothing goes right. I can't be sure what is running through Simon Peter's mind, but I had experienced such thoughts as a minister of the Gospel when I decided the ministry was not working. "I'll go back to doing what I did before I did this ministry gig," I remember such a time and even called my brother Richard and asked if I could have a job working for him. (By the way, Richard is a wonderful, godly, and wise man who told me, "Nah, you stay with the pastorate; it will all work out." He was right, of course.)

I absolutely love how Jesus refused to leave Earth without healing Simon Peter. Peter's relationship with Jesus was the cause of Peter's severe inner injuries. Yes, Peter had picked his words and actions poorly. Yes, Jesus had warned Peter. Yes, Peter's sins and choices caused his guilt and pain. Peter picked poorly. Jesus was not going to leave him that way! He will not leave you injured either, my friend. Yes, sometimes we feel, "I am afraid that I'm just one mistake away from You leaving me this way?" He loves you. When He said He would never leave or forsake us, Jesus also cared about you and me.

"When the sun came up, Jesus was standing on the beach, but they didn't recognize him. Jesus spoke to them: "Good morning! Did you catch anything for breakfast?" They answered, "No." He said, "Throw the net off the right side of the boat and see what happens." They did what he said. Suddenly there were so many fish in it, and they weren't strong enough to pull it in. Then the disciple Jesus loved said to Peter, "It's the Master!" When Simon Peter realized that it was the Master, he threw on some clothes, for he was stripped for work and dove into the sea. The other disciples came in by boat, for they weren't far from land, a hundred yards or so, pulling along the net full of fish. When they got out of the boat, they saw a fire laid, with fish and bread cooking on it. Jesus said, "Bring some of the fish you've just caught." Simon Peter joined them and pulled the net to shore—153 big fish! And even with all those fish, the net didn't rip. Jesus said, "Breakfast is ready." Not one of the disciples dared ask, "Who are you?" They knew it was the Master. Jesus then took the bread and gave it to them. He did the same with the fish. This was now the third time Jesus had shown himself alive to the disciples since being raised from the dead. After breakfast, Jesus asked Simon Peter, "Simon, son of John, do you love me more than these?" "Yes, Master, you know I love you. "Jesus said, "Feed my lambs." He then asked a second time, "Simon, son of John, do you love me?" "Yes, Master, you know I love you." Jesus said, "Shepherd, my sheep." Then he said it a third time: "Simon, son of John, do you love me?" Peter was upset that he asked for the third time, "Do you love me?" so he answered, "Master, you know everything there is to know. You've got to know that I love you." Jesus said, "Feed my sheep. I'm telling you the very truth now..... "Follow me."

I call this Peter's "Restoration Breakfast." When Jesus predicted Peter's failure, remember that He also said, " I have prayed for you that you may not lose your faith. Yes, when you have turned back to me, you must strengthen these brothers of yours." Jesus is helping Peter "turn back to me." But Peter needs Jesus' healing. It starts with Jesus' prayer for him, "I have prayed that you may not lose your faith." Let me ask you, who prayed for you that you would not be lost in eternity? Who refused that picture? My parents and grandparents called out my name in prayer to the Lord and others. Who do you and I pray for? Who are we standing in the gap for?

Jesus then leads Peter through three restoration question-and-answer processes. One for each of Peter's denials. "When they had finished breakfast, Jesus said to Simon Peter, "Simon, son of John, do you love Me more than these [others do—with total commitment and devotion]?" He said to Him, "Yes, Lord; You know that I [b]love You [with a deep, personal affection, as for a close friend]." Jesus said to him, "Feed My lambs." Notice the Amplified Bible points out the differences in the love words that appear in this healing conversation. Jesus uses "Agape," defined as "with total commitment and devotion," and I would add intentional reasoning. Peter responds with "Phileo" "with a deep, personal affection, as for a close friend." Did Jesus get the answer He wanted? Some have said that Jesus is asking Peter to love (Agape) Him as more than just a friend (Phileo). Jesus challenges him to "Feed my Lambs," clearly identifying his call to the leadership of His church. Jesus repeats the question, and Peter repeats his friendship answer. Jesus responds with, "Shepherd, My Sheep." The third time Jesus switches to Peter's choice verb of friendship. "Peter was grieved that He asked him the third time, "Do you [really] [c]love Me [with a deep, personal affection, as for a close friend]?" And he said to Him, "Lord, You know everything; You know that I love You [with a deep, personal affection, as for a close friend]." Jesus said to him, "Feed My sheep." Healing our hearts can be terribly painful, which shows in this repeated love-questioning process. Did Jesus get the answer He wanted? By the time Acts 2, 4, and 5 rolled around, He certainly did. In Acts 2, Peter is filled with the Holy Spirit. Three thousand gave their lives to Christ as Peter preached. He is not the confused, injured, "I am going fishing for the fish guy" now! As Jesus predicted, he is a "Fisher of Men and Women." He is bold, self-assured, Christ-confident, and so full of Jesus that the "Who's Who" crowd of religious leaders in Acts 4 think of Jesus when Peter is in the room with them. In Acts 5, people are laying the sick people along the streets so that Peter's shadow will fall on them to be healed when he walks by. Wow! That's a long way from his answer to the servant girl, "I don't know Him."

Sometimes in our walk, we all need a "Restoration Breakfast" to heal our hearts, minds, and emotions. Sometimes it is our own self-inflicted injuries. Other times someone or life's circumstance has injured us. Me? I have needed this healing many times. When you are saying "Yes!" to Him and living out the "Committed Beyond Choice" lifestyle, and you are injured, or in trouble, He will not leave you that way. He will not!

Restoration Breakfast

1. Healing Prayer (Luke 22:32) "I have prayed for you that you may not lose your faith. Yes, when you have turned back to me, you must strengthen these brothers of yours."
2. Three Restoration Questions and Answers (John 21:15-17)

Question	Question	Question
"Simon son of John, do you love (agape) me more than these?"	"Simon son of John, do you love (agape) me?"	"Simon son of John, do you love (phileo) me?"
Answer	**Answer**	**Answer**
"Yes, Lord," he said, "you know that I love (phileo) you."	"Yes, Lord, you know that I love (phileo) you."	"Lord, you know all things; you know that I love (phileo) you."
Reply	**Reply**	**Reply**
"Feed my lambs."	"Shepherd my sheep."	"Feed my sheep."

Reflection and Discussion Questions

1. Why do you think Simon Peter failed? What led up to his "Triple Denial?"

2. What do you observe and describe Simon Peter's response to his own "Triple Denial?"

3. What was the response of the other disciples to Simon Peter's self-inflicted injury?

4. What do you notice about Jesus' "Restoration Breakfast" process?

5. How can we learn and practice Jesus' approach to a friend suffered an injury to their inner heart?

6. Have you ever needed or still need a "Restoration Breakfast?" Describe that need.
7. Close in praying for your group and again for your 3rd chair loved ones.

Notes

_____

_____

_____

_____

_____

_____

_____

_____

_____

_____

Chapter Seven
"Gary, Let that be a Lesson to you." Part 1

What I don't understand about myself is that I decide one way, but then I act another, doing things I absolutely despise. Romans 7:15 MSG

I had lost it! Carol and I were newly married and living the life of an evangelist/revivalist. In that day, our early twenties (1971-1975), we would travel to churches and communities that invited us, and we would do services each day or night for a week, at least twice on Sundays and sometimes more, ten days (usually a Wednesday through two Sundays) or sometimes a weekend. Carol would play the piano, and she and I would lead worship music. Then in between congregational hymns and choruses, I would sing solos with her at the keyboard. We were still experiencing the great movement of God that had started with the Asbury College Revival of 1070. We expected God's power to touch and change lives when we ministered. He did. As I have said, "He Just Showed Up!"[43] He did transform and change lives wherever He sent us. We boast of Him only in that thousands came to Christ during the period of the February 3, 1970 revival until we accepted a church plant pastorate in October 1975.

It was during this time we hit a snag, a spiritual dry spell. There just wasn't the Presence of the Lord in the services like we had been experiencing. It was especially noticeable to us during the music and worship times. Music was not my most vital area of skill or of spiritual giftedness. On the other hand, Carol was a highly trained, skilled, and spiritually gifted musician. When she played the piano, you felt the Presence of the Lord.

So, what was the problem? The problem was me. I had allowed some habitual sin to creep into my life. It had been there for several weeks. It reminds me of this story from Joshua:

Remember the biblical story of Ai? Joshua had just taken over the leadership of Israel from the now-

---

[43] Gary E. Wright. *He Just Showed Up: An Eyewitness to Revival.* Amazon. 2021.

deceased Moses. In Joshua 6, the famous battle of Jericho takes place and God's power is on display. Even Elvis sang, "Joshua fought the battle of Jericho, and the walls came tumbling down. "Joshua's leadership is credited with the "W," but it was raw GOD power knocking down the massive protective walls of that greatly fortified city. God used Joshua as His leadership tool, constantly reminding him, "Be strong and courageous, for you are the one who will lead these people to possess all the land I swore to their ancestors I would give them."[44]

The next city of challenge for Israel was the little town of Ai (which means *Ruin*). It was very small, and all predicted an easy win after Israel conquered the mighty walled and protected city of Jericho. They failed! They failed miserably. Israel's soldiers "fled in defeat before the men of Ai! The men of Ai killed thirty-six— chased them from the city gate as far as the Quarries, killing them at the descent. The heart of the people sank, all spirit knocked out of them."[45] A humiliated new leader, Joshua, has a meltdown in his prayer closet, "Joshua ripped his clothes and fell on his face to the ground before the Chest of God, he and the leaders throwing dirt on their heads, prostrate until evening. Joshua said, "Oh, oh, oh .[].[]. Master, God. Why did you insist on bringing this people across the Jordan? To make us victims of the Amorites? To wipe us out?." "But the Lord said to Joshua, "Get up! Why are you lying on your face like this? Israel has sinned and broken my covenant!"[46] What was the problem? They had an "I" (Ai) problem.[47] One person had caused defeat when

---

[44] Joshua 1 NLT

[45] Joshua 7 MSG

[46] Joshua 7:10 NLT.

[47] In recovery ministries we learned we must remind ourselves to stop blaming and shaming others and take responsibility for our sin and poor choices. David said in his prayer of repentance in Psalm 51 NLT, "Against you, and you alone,

they chose something saying, "I want it!" and took that which was sacred to the Lord. God had withheld his power from Israel because of sin. On their second try, after ridding themselves of the sin, they easily won the battle. One person in sin can hinder a whole group! It made the whole nation powerless. A small army ran, and they blamed God for their defeat. We often blame and shame God when it is our poor choice or sin that causes problems. Right?

Most men and women fall over sin in some form of one of three areas, money, sex, or power, "throughout history and in our own experience, these issues seem inseparably intertwined. Money manifests itself as power. And power is often called 'the best aphrodisiac'."[48] Foster goes on to say, "Historically, it seems that spiritual revivals have been accompanied by clear, bold responses to the issues of money, sex, and power."[49] The Ai story is about materialism, money.

My dad often was scheduled with Carol and me to do the services or sometimes I just invited him to help us. During this season of struggle, he had served with us. He would preach one night; I would do the next. Carol and I would do the worship music. One particular night we were serving in a little town in Ohio. I preached. I do believe my scripture text was given to me by the Lord. It was the confrontation between David and his pastor, Nathan.

> Pastor Nathan told King David, "There were two men in the same city—one rich, the other poor. The rich man had huge flocks of sheep, herds of cattle. The poor man had nothing but one little female lamb, which he had bought and raised. It grew up with him and his children as a member of the family. It ate off his plate and drank from his cup and slept on his bed. It was like a daughter to him.

---

have I sinned; I have done what is evil in your sight." He had an "I" problem.
[48] Foster, *Richard. Money, Sex and Power: The Challenge of the Disciplined Life.* London: Great Britain, 1985. 2.
[49] Ibid.3.

One day a traveler dropped in on the rich man. He was too stingy to take an animal from his own herds or flocks to make a meal for his visitor, so he took the poor man's lamb and prepared a meal to set before his guest. David exploded in anger. "As surely as God lives," he said to Nathan, "the man who did this ought to be lynched! He must repay for the lamb four times over for his crime and his stinginess!" "You're the man!" said Nathan. [Samuel Brengel observes, "This divine courage will surely accompany the fiery Baptism of the Spirit.[50]] "And here's what God, the God of Israel, has to say to you: I made you king over Israel. I freed you from the fist of Saul. I gave you your master's daughter and other wives to have and to hold. I gave you both Israel and Judah. And if that hadn't been enough, I'd have gladly thrown in much more. So why have you treated the word of God with brazen contempt, doing this great evil? You murdered Uriah the Hittite, then took his wife as your wife. Worse, you killed him with an Ammonite sword! And now, because you treated God with such contempt and took Uriah the Hittite's wife as your wife, killing and murder will continually plague your family."

Now as I was preaching and read, "You're the man!" It was like the big finger of God turned and pointed right back at me! Many people crowded around the altar that night to get rid of sin, and I was one of them. As I invited people to an altar of confession, I confessed to them that I also needed to repent. I remember praying aggressively, loudly, and long. Finally, the witness of peace came. I was so exhausted. I got up from the altar and sat in the chair behind the podium. My dad and others prayed with all the people at the altar as Carol softly played appropriate hymns and choruses at the piano. This "Afterglow" time is my favorite time of worship. Interestingly, God still used my primary gift of preaching, but my secondary gift in music suffered. God still used me, but I was not as efficient tool as before. How often, like Samson, do we

---

[50] Brengle, Samuel Logan. *The Collected Works of SL Brengle - Eight books in one* (p. 479). Jawbone Digital. Kindle Edition.

mistake God's Presence in our lives during sinful behaviors and conclude we are fine? Only to wake up one day, like Samson and the electrical power of the Spirit has been shut off! After a while of praying and counseling people, my dad came and sat beside me. In that moment, I sensed that the Lord wanted me to share a song, so I whispered the title to Carol, and she began to play the keyboard, and I sang the song. This time as I sang, and for the first time in weeks, the Presence of the Lord filled the room during the music. Nothing compares to such *Presence In the Midst*[51] moments when *He Shows Up*. I so enjoyed His Presence as I sang. I was also relieved that He was back in my life that way. As the song ended, I sat back down next to my dad. Dad had said nothing to me about my problem over the recent weeks, even though it had been a hindrance to him and Carol. Then, he reached over, squeezed my knee, looked me right in the eye, and said, "Now, son, let that teach you a lesson. Don't ever lose the Anointing again. It's the most precious possession you will ever have. "Looking back 50 years later, dad was so right. Nothing compares to His Presence and anointing in our lives. " He doesn't treat us as our sins deserve, nor pay us back in full for our wrongs. As high as heaven is over the earth, so strong is his love to those who fear him. I'm sure glad "God's power shows up best in weak people."[52] I easily qualify, how about you?

Question? What was that "Anointing" my dad was talking about? What does the Bible say about it? What do Godly people say about it?

Jesus used the term during his first sermon in His hometown synagogue, Nazareth. "He came to Nazareth, where he had been raised. As he always did on the Sabbath, he went to the meeting place. When he stood up to read, he was handed the scroll of the prophet Isaiah. Unrolling the scroll, he found the place where it was written, "When he came to the village of Nazareth, his boyhood home, he went as usual to the synagogue on the Sabbath and stood up to read the Scriptures. The scroll of Isaiah the prophet was handed to him. He unrolled the scroll

---

[51] *The Presence in the Midst*, by James Doyle Penrose (Mitchelstown, Dublin 1864 – Bognor Regis 1932). A famous Quaker artwork showing the silhouette of Christ hovering over a congregation in worship.
[52] 2 Corinthians 12:9 LBT.

and found the place where this was written: "The Spirit of the Lord is upon me, for he has *anointed* [(Greek word *chriō*) consecrating Jesus to the Messianic office and furnishing him with the necessary powers for its administration] me to bring Good News to the poor. He has sent me to proclaim that captives will be released, that the blind will see, that the oppressed will be set free, and that the time of the Lord's favor has come." He rolled up the scroll, handed it back to the attendant, and sat down. All eyes in the synagogue looked at him intently. Then he began to speak to them. "The Scripture you've just heard has been fulfilled this very day!"[53]

Jesus was quoting Isaiah 61, "The Spirit of the Sovereign Lord is upon me, for the Lord has *anointed* me to bring good news to the poor." Isaiah used the Old Testament Hebrew word *māšaḥ* (מָשַׁח verb, to smear, anoint, spread a liquid or to anoint, consecrate). This was the word describing the occasions when Samuel proclaimed Saul and David Kings of Israel. "Then Samuel took a flask of olive oil and poured it on Saul's head and kissed him, saying, "Has not the Lord *anointed* you, ruler, over his inheritance."[54] "The Spirit of the Lord will come powerfully upon you, and you will prophesy...As Saul turned to leave Samuel, God changed Saul's heart, and all these signs were fulfilled that day....the Spirit of God came powerfully upon him."[55] "So Samuel took the horn of oil and anointed him in the presence of his brothers, and from that day on, the Spirit of the Lord came powerfully upon David."[56]

Notice that in all three instances where the word and action of "anointing" are used, the phrase "the Spirit of the Lord is upon him" is stated in some form. This "anointing" is to usher a person into the office of a King or with Jesus the Messiah. But it is also to give the spiritual power to enable, administrate, or carry out the calling of their position. "Not by might nor by power, but by my Spirit,' says the Lord Almighty."[57]

---

[53] Luke 4:16-20 NLT
[54] 1 Samuel 10:1 NIV
[55] Ibid., 5-10.
[56] ! Samuel 16:13 NIV
[57] Zechariah 4:6 NIV.

Exodus 29 records the "anointing" (the same word used for the Kings) to consecrate worship accessory objects, clothes of the priests, Aaron, and the priests. It was the ointment, the holy oil used in the consecration of the Aaronic priests.[58] Objects and people were consecrated[59], set aside, for a particular function or use by God.

Therefore, this "anointing" is an installation of an office, a setting aside of a person or thing just for God's work. Still, more importantly for our study, the actual enablement by the Holy Spirit, "the Spirit of the Lord is upon me." Jesus said,(*I like to use the Amplified Version here to help us get the meaning of the phrases*) "The Spirit of the Lord [is] upon Me, because He has *anointed* Me [the Anointed One, the Messiah] to preach the good news (the Gospel) to the poor(poor in Spirit meaning those seeking God[60]); He has sent Me to announce release to the captives and recovery of sight to the blind, to send forth as delivered those who are oppressed [who are downtrodden, bruised, crushed, and broken down by calamity], To proclaim the accepted and acceptable year of the Lord [the day when salvation and the free favors of God profusely abound].

Jesus' job description (Isaiah 61, Luke 4), Anointed to:

-Be Sent by the Father

-Proclaim Good News (the Gospel) to the poor in Spirit, meaning those seeking God.

-Announce release to the captives

-Recover sight to the blind

---

[58] Blue Letter Bible App. https://www.blueletterbible.org/lexicon/h4888/kjv/wlc/0-1/

[59] Ibid., אֵלֻּמ millu', mil-loo'; from; a fulfilling (only in plural), i.e. (literally) a setting (of gems), or (technically) consecration (also concretely, a dedicatory sacrifice):—consecration, be set.

[60] My translation of "poor"

- deliver those who are oppressed, who are downtrodden, bruised, crushed, and broken down by calamity

-Proclaim and Purchase Salvation as God's Gift of Grace

Notice also the number of times in this chapter we are told Jesus was "filled with the Spirit." The chapter begins, "Then Jesus, full of and controlled by the Holy Spirit, returned from the Jordan and was led in [by] the [Holy] Spirit."[61] After the Temptation, it states, "Then Jesus went back full of and under the power of the [Holy] Spirit into Galilee."[62] In the synagogue itself, Jesus publicly states, "The Spirit of the Lord is upon Me" and then connects it to He "has anointed me to."

It should be noted that this "anointing" has to do with the power of the Spirit of the Lord, which comes upon and in human beings to do the work of the ministry. It's about Power, God's Power. In Acts 10, the Apostle Simon Peter states, " You know the contents of the message which He (Jesus) sent to Israel, announcing the good news (Gospel) of peace by Jesus Christ, Who is Lord of all— The [same] message which was proclaimed throughout all Judea, starting from Galilee after the baptism preached by John— How God anointed and consecrated Jesus of Nazareth with the [Holy] Spirit and with strength and ability and power; how He went about doing good and, in particular, curing all who were harassed and oppressed by [the power of] the devil, for God was with Him. And we are [eye and ear] witnesses of everything that He did both in the land of the Jews and in Jerusalem." [63] Observe the description of the anointing by the Amplified Version translators, " with the [Holy] Spirit and with strength and ability and power." Eugene Peterson's translation states, "anointed by God with the Holy Spirit.. He was able to do all this because God was with him."[64]

---

[61] Luke 4 AMPC
[62] Ibid.
[63] Acts 10:36-40 AMPC
[64] Ibid. MSG

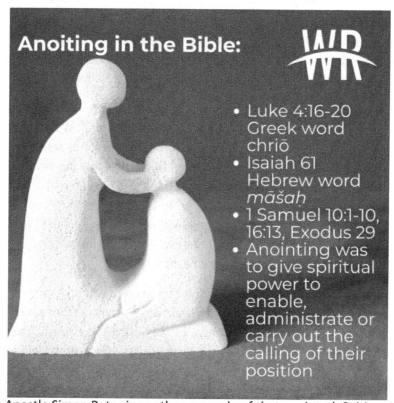

Anoiting in the Bible:

- Luke 4:16-20 Greek word chriō
- Isaiah 61 Hebrew word *māšaḥ*
- 1 Samuel 10:1-10, 16:13, Exodus 29
- Anointing was to give spiritual power to enable, administrate or carry out the calling of their position

The Apostle Simon Peter is another example of that anointed, Spirit-filled dynamic. In the last chapter of John, Jesus challenges him with, "Do you really love Me." Turn the page to Acts 2, and a Spirit-filled Simon Peter preached to the same city, some of the same crowd that witnessed his denial of Jesus, and 3000 became Christ's followers! When arrested and placed before the religious and political "Who's Who" crowd of the Jewish nation in Acts 4, we find, "Then Peter, [because he was] filled with [and controlled by] the Holy Spirit," spoke boldly about Jesus as the Messiah and stated they had rejected the Messiah. He spoke with skill. "13 Now when they saw the boldness and unfettered eloquence of Peter and John and perceived that they were unlearned and untrained in the schools [common men with no educational advantages], they marveled; and they recognized that they had been with Jesus." Folks, this was more than Jesus' training (they had been with Jesus) of Simon Peter, and John. The Spirit of the Lord Himself was now inside the Jewish body of Simon Peter! He, Jesus, was in that room with them all! Turn another page, Acts 5:17, and people "kept carrying out the sick into the streets and placing them on couches and sleeping pads, [in the hope] that as Peter passed by, at least his shadow might fall on some of them." Anointing, power from the "Spirit of the Lord."

I have learned about we preachers and teachers of the Word that the anointing of the Spirit should not be presumed. We cannot presume the Presence of the Lord is upon us just because we have accepted a calling, studied the Bible and ministry, given diplomas and degrees, and are teaching or preaching the Word. Yes, the Word comes with its own anointing. "So shall My word be that goes forth out of My mouth: it shall not return to Me void [without producing any effect, useless], but it shall accomplish that which I please and purpose, and it shall prosper in the thing for which I sent it."[65]

Nevertheless, we all have tried to listen to someone preach or teach the Word and can't stay with them as listeners. At times one wonders, "How can they make the Bible so boring?" Obviously, there can be many reasons a person is dry and boring when attempting to teach or preach. At some time or another, I failed for all the reasons we could list. Should we just accept that the style, lack of preparation, poor skills of the messenger are the reasons most in the audience are daydreaming and thinking of something else? Is that consistent with biblical examples of God's speaking to human beings through His messengers. After all, "And the Lord opened the mouth of the donkey, and she said to Balaam, 'What have I done to you that you should strike me these three times?"[66] I don't think that was the last time a donkey tried to give the Word of God. Just say'n...

It's not just the speakers of the Word, Churches; congregations should have the anointing, the "Spirit of the Lord upon them." One of my former staff, former because she is now in heaven, had drifted from God as a teenager of 16. When she was the mother of a 16-year-old daughter who was in trouble, she finally accepted the invitation of her dental hygienist to church. She described to me that first Sunday, "We

---

[65] Isaiah 55:11 AMPC
[66] Numbers 22: 28 AMPC

were late. My daughter and I entered the church hallway. We heard music. I felt It. I thought, 'Now I remember, that's what God feels like!" She explained that she had forgotten what the Presence of the Lord felt like. She had known that Presence growing up in church. She had been away from any church for over 30 years. The moment she entered this Spirit-filled, anointed church, she recognized the Presence in the Midst. Soon, she was on her knees at the altar with her daughter confessing her sin and returning to following Christ, now for the first time as an adult. Another friend states he attended church for 50 years and hated it. His wife talked him into attending her church with her, the same church in the previous story. He states that the first Sunday, he *felt* the Presence of the Lord and wondered, "What have I been missing all these years?" Now, he and his wife, children, and grandchildren hardly ever miss. Just this week, another woman who had not been following Christ told her son about the same church, "It's not the music, it's not the preachers when I walk through the door, I feel God, I don't want to miss church."

Dr. Dennis Kinlaw was the President of Asbury College during the great revival of 1970. He was a great preacher and teacher and became my friend later in our lives. About anointed preachers, he said, " As I read the biblical biographies of mighty preachers, I'm convinced that ultimately there is no great preaching unless the preacher partakes of the divine holiness in some measure. While worldliness may make a preacher clever, it will never make him powerful. The Spirit of the Lord within us can reach someone else with the gospel far more effectively than we can reach that person in our own persuasive eloquence. Our ministry must come out of our walk with God."

Kinlaw continues, "Our perpetual temptation in the ministry is to let the ministry take priority over our personal walk with Christ. We are always conscious of the pressures to put the work first. That is so easy to justify. The reality, though, is that we always move from serving in his resources, gained from intimacy with him, to ministry that arises from our own strength alone. Our security against such a drift is the development of personal devotional habits that keep him central and that maintain a perpetual influx of his life and power. We must know the resurrected Christ and commune with him each day. [67]

If one has ever known that Presence, he is also aware that he can lose it. At pastors conferences the most common concern was the fact that the Presence they once had known was now lost. The joy, the excitement, the drama of the ministry was gone because they had lost the sense of Christ's Presence amid the pressure of their work."[68] Church leaders are human. If they struggle, as stated earlier, it is usually in the areas of money, sex, or power, sometimes, all three, like Solomon. God gifted Samson to protect Israel, "At that moment, the Spirit of the Lord came powerfully upon him, and he ripped the lion's jaws apart with his bare hands." Samson lost the power but not all at once. His apparent weakness was sex, but fame and power were associated with how God used him even though he sinned and the power of God remained in his life. Finally, "When he woke up, he thought, "I will do as before and shake myself free." But he didn't realize the Lord had left him."[69]

Here seems to be an issue that leaders often fool themselves with. "For God's gifts and His call are irrevocable. [He never withdraws them when once they are given, and He does not change His mind about those to whom He gives His grace or to whom He sends His call.]" We leaders sin, but some form of the Presence, anointing, remains in our lives and so conclude, think we have gotten by with it, or our sin is somehow not so bad. God is merciful. However, if we continue our ways, like Samson, or King Saul, we eventually will wake up and "he did not realize the Lord had left him."

My family, and my leadership development, have taught me to conclude that if there is this "anointing," the Presence, the Power, "the Spirit of the Lord is upon me," it is because of a price paid that would ensure my intimacy with Christ. This worship and offering of our lives, the "Yes!" makes the difference. The iconic passage is Paul's Romans 12, "So, here's what I want you to do, God helping you: Take your everyday, ordinary life—your sleeping, eating, going-to-work, and walking-around life—and place it before God as an offering. Embracing what God does for you is the best thing you can do for him. Don't become so well-

---

[67] Romans 11:29 AMPC.
[68] Kinlaw, Dennis F.. Preaching in the Spirit . Warner Press Inc.. Kindle Edition.
[69] Judges 16:20. NLT.

adjusted to your culture that you fit into it without even thinking. Instead, fix your attention on God. You'll be changed from the inside out."[70]

The Gospel of Mark described Jesus' method and best practice with the Apostles, "He climbed a mountain and invited those he wanted with him. They climbed together. He settled on twelve and designated them, apostles. The plan was that they would *be with Him,* and he would send them out to proclaim the Word and give them authority to banish demons."[71] Did you catch that, the plan? "The plan was that *they would be with Him.*"[72] We tend to focus on "sending them out," and "proclaiming the Word," and fighting demons.

First and foremost, we must be with Him. We will have no power but human power if we do not spend time with Him, absorbing Him. We need God power, not manpower. Paul cried out in his last public letter, "I want to know Christ." By this time, his ministry was almost over. The death sentence had been cast; he's on death row. What is the old Apostle's main concern? More of you, Jesus! More of you!

Refection and Discussion Questions

1. Have you ever experienced a "dry" time spiritually? What helped you feel 'refreshed' and ready to proceed forward?
2. Who is a mentor or spiritual advisor that you depend on to help you with your spiritual walk?
3. What is your observation of the author's, "let that be a lesson to you," that can teach others?
4. Describe your understanding of the "anointing."
5. What do you consider the author's action plan to be in this chapter?
6. Close in praying for your group and again for your 3rd chair loved ones.

---

[70] Romans 12:1-2 MSG.
[71] Mark 3 MSG
[72] Philippians 3.

Notes

_____

_____

_____

_____

_____

_____

_____

_____

_____

_____

_____

Chapter Eight
The Anointed Part 2

But letting the Spirit control your mind leads to life and peace.

Dr. Dennis Kinlaw tells this wonderful story:

> One of my heroes is a man who never graduated from college. However, he may be as smart as anyone I have ever met. His Christian influence has reached around the world. The key to his life was a conversation with Lettie Cowman, author of Streams in the Desert,* who shared with my friend the determinative experience of her life. When she and her husband, Charles Cowman,[73] were new Christians, they attended a missionary conference led by A. B. Simpson, founder of the Christian and Missionary Alliance Church. When Dr. Simpson finished his message, he said, "Folks, God is here. We must take an offering. This will be an unusual offering. You will notice that the offering plates are not empty. They are full of watches. These watches are not gold, but they are good watches. If you will put your gold watch in the plate, you may take one of these cheaper watches. We will sell your gold watch and send the message of Christ to those who do not know it." When the plate came to Lettie, she handed it to her husband. To her shock, he took the plate, placed in it his gold watch that she had given him, and took out one of the cheaper watches. She reproachfully said, "I gave that to you." But the plate was gone.

---

[73] Charles Elmer Cowman (March 13, 1868 – September 25, 1924) was a missionary evangelist in Japan. He was also one of the cofounders of the Oriental Missionary Society (now One Mission Society; formerly OMS International).

Dr. Simpson then said, "Folks, God is here. We must take another offering. This time the plates will be empty. Many of us wear more jewelry than is necessary for good grooming. If you will put the jewelry which you really don't need in the plate, we will sell it and send the message of Christ to those that do not know it." When the plate came to Lettie, she handed it to her husband. He took the plate with his left hand, then reached over with his right hand and slipped her engagement ring off her finger. He placed it in the plate. Horrified, she said, "You gave that to me." But the plate was gone.

Then Dr. Simpson said, "Folks, God is here. Now we must take a money offering." When the plate came, she handed it to her husband and watched as her husband took from his pocket an envelope containing his paycheck for the previous two weeks. He put it in the plate. She said to him, "How are we going to buy groceries?" But the plate was gone.

Then Dr. Simpson said, "Folks, God is here. Now we must take the real offering, the offering of life. If you will give your life to carry the gospel to the world, stand up." Lettie Cowman's husband stood. Lettie said, "It was the determining moment of my life. I knew that if my husband said he was going, he would go whether I went with him or not. So, I stood." The impact of that story on my friend was such that he decided that he must give his life totally to Christ and live it totally for him. He did not become a preacher. He has spent his entire life as a businessman who lives to witness for Christ. The result is that his influence has been more extensive across the world and more fruitful in souls than that of anyone else I know. It is wonderful what God does when he gets all of one of us. [74]

[74] Kinlaw, Dennis F.. This Day with the Master (Discovery Devotional Series) . Zondervan. Kindle Edition. Lettie (Mrs. Charles E.) Cowman, Streams in the

I have noticed this trend of spiritual focus on the anointed old preachers in my life. As their years enter the winter seasons of their lives, they are predictable on the topics of their talks. "Today, I want to talk to you about being filled with the Holy Spirit," the old preacher said. Merl Roe, that old preacher, had the entire Bible memorized; he could have spoken eloquently on any topic in the scriptures. However, I had predicted his topic for the college students that day. It was mostly what he talked about every time I heard him. My earthly father was the same. Could it be that at these late years of their lives, like the Apostle Paul, they realized the conclusion that the only chance we have as the church to change this world is "having the Spirit of the Lord upon" us?

It's an old, old hymn, yet the words and lyrics speak to our subject of anointing and intimacy with Christ.

More About Jesus Would I know.

1

More about Jesus would I know,
More of His grace to others show;
More of His saving fulness see,
More of His love who died for me.

Chorus: More, more about Jesus,
More, more about Jesus;
More of His saving fulness see,
More of His love who died for me.

2

More about Jesus let me learn,
More of His holy will discern;
Spirit of God my teacher be,
Showing the things of Christ to me.

3

More about Jesus; in His Word,
Holding communion with my Lord;
Hearing His voice in every line,
Making each faithful saying mine.

Desert (Los Angeles: Oriental Missionary Society, 1925).

4

More about Jesus; on His throne,
Riches in glory all His own.
More of His kingdom's sure increase.
More of His coming, Prince of Peace.[75]

Notice the 3rd stanza it not just knowing about Jesus: "Holding communion with my Lord.
Hearing His voice in every line, Making each faithful saying mine."

It's about knowing Him. I'm right with Moses when God passed by, and Moses' response was "Own us, possess us!" I was still a teenager when I wrote in my Bible and later in my journal, "The power and anointing of God in my life is in direct measurement to my surrender to Christ." I did not read that anywhere; I could see it in people's lives one way or another. I don't know how much I understood then.

What is it I need to surrender to in Christ? My priority must be my schedule to spend time with Him. My first priority must be time with Him and obedience to what He says. My job description? Say, "YES! to Him." "Search me, O God, and know my heart; test me and know my anxious thoughts. Point out anything in me that offends you and leads me along the path of everlasting life. Psalm 139: 23-24. The longer I live, the less I trust me, and the more I trust Him.

My second priority is to spend time with my wife. She is a wonderful helpmate to me. I hope I am to her. The Apostle Simon Peter wrote about her when he said, "In the same way, you husbands must give honor to your wives. Treat your wife with understanding as you live together. She may be weaker than you are, but she is your equal partner in God's gift of new life. Treat her as you should so your prayers will not be hindered." How can I treat my wife with understanding if I don't spend time with her just like I won't understand Him if I won't

---

[75] More about Jesus would I know, More of his grace to others show
Author: E. E. Hewitt (1887)
Tune: SWENEY (Sweney).

spend time with Him. My prayers, yes my anointing will "be hindered" if I am not treating her right.

Observe you do not need to be a preacher or teacher to need the anointing. Bezalel is first in Bible to be named as "filled him with the Spirit of the God, with skill, ability and knowledge in all kinds of crafts to make artistic designs for work." for the purpose of the designing and building the Tabernacle.[76] What gift did God give you? The Holy Spirit wants to empower that gift in you with His Spirit. As Jesus taught later for all of His followers, "And I will ask the Father, and he will give you another Advocate, who will never leave you. He is the Holy Spirit, who leads into all truth. The world cannot receive him because it isn't looking for him and doesn't recognize him. But you know him because he lives with you now and later will be in you. No, I will not abandon you as orphans—I will come to you."
Peter wrote, "But you are a chosen people, a royal priesthood, a holy nation, God's special possession, that you may declare the praises of him who called you out of darkness into his wonderful light."[77]

Whatever your spiritual giftedness, it is to further and support the spread of the Good News of Jesus the Christ. "So, if you're serious about living this new resurrection life with Christ, act like it. Pursue (some translations say "seek") the things over which Christ presides. Don't shuffle along, eyes to the ground, absorbed with the things right in front of you. Look up and be alert to what is going on around Christ— that's where the action is. See things from his perspective."[78] John Rhinehart said about this passage:

"The word seek in this context means "to devote serious effort to realize one's desire or objective." Athletes devote serious effort in order to win a race. Farmers devote serious effort in order to harvest a big crop. Soldiers devote serious effort in order to win a battle. And Christians are called to

---

[76] Exodus 35:30-35 NLT
[77] 1 Peter 2:9 NIV.
[78] Colossians 3:1-2. MSG

devote serious effort in order to advance Jesus' kingdom. William Wilberforce nailed this when he wrote, "No one expects to attain to the height of learning, or arts, or power, or wealth, or military glory, without vigorous resolution and strenuous diligence, and steady perseverance. Yet we expect to be Christians without labor, study, or inquiry. The Bible is clear: we are not saved only to relax, retire, and wait for heaven. We are saved by grace, but saved to works. After God saves us He intends to use us in His work on earth."[79]

I have a friend; he had been a lifelong alcoholic. I introduced him to the Lord 22 years ago. He is a gifted businessman. He is not a preacher, but he is filled with the Spirit and empowered to produce funding so that the Gospel is preached globally. He is the one who introduced me to John Rhinehart and *Gospel Patrons.* [80] I would say he is an anointed producer of creating funds to support the spread of the Gospel message. He also has the gift of serving and hospitality. He is the hands and feet of Jesus this way. At the present he has built or in the process of building four recovery houses for men and women to recover from substance abuse. He loves doing business like I love preaching. It takes this kind of partnership to get the job of the Kingdom done.

After the Resurrection, the Twelve were hiding and meeting behind locked doors in fear that what happened to Jesus might happen to them. Then Jesus walked through the walls and said, "Peace be with you! As the Father has sent me, I am sending you." And with that he breathed on them and said, "Receive the Holy Spirit."[81] "During the forty days after his crucifixion, he appeared to the apostles from time to time, and he proved to them in many ways that he was actually alive. And he talked to them about the Kingdom of God."[82] Are not those wonderful words? "He breathed on them," the Breath of

---

[79]

Rinehart, John. *Gospel Patrons* (p. 156-157). Reclaimed Publishing. Kindle Edition.
[80] Ibid.
[81] John 20:21-22. NLT.
[82] Acts 1 MSG

Heaven. He knew He could never teach or train these men in the forty days He had left on earth without this special anointing of the Spirit. So, they received the Pre-Pentecost Holy Spirit experience enabling Him to pass the Kingdom of God baton to them. It included several one-on-one conversations with Him and Peter, James, Mary Magalia. There were small group sessions and healings like Thomas and Peter. "Once when he was eating with them, he commanded them, "Do not leave Jerusalem until the Father sends you the gift he promised, as I told you before, John baptized with[water], but in just a few days you will be baptized with the Holy Spirit." "But you will receive power when the Holy Spirit comes upon you. And you will be my witnesses, telling people about me everywhere—in Jerusalem, throughout Judea, in Samaria, and to the ends of the earth." Then He left. Whatever of the Holy Spirit they got in their "Pre-Pentecost" "Breath of Heaven" was just the beginning. He was saying, I promise, I have a lot more for you! Do not leave town without it!" They did not leave town without it! They got it! They pass it on to thousands at Pentecost and eventually on to us! Peter's Pentecost sermon stated, "Change your life. Turn to God and be baptized, each of you, in the name of Jesus Christ, so your sins are forgiven. Receive the gift of the Holy Spirit. The promise is targeted to you and your children, but also to all who are far away—whomever, in fact, our Master God invites."[83] How powerful was this sermon? "Peter's words pierced their hearts, and they said to him and to the other apostles, "Brothers, what should we do?" "Those who believed what Peter said were baptized and added to the church that day—about 3,000 in all." Soon the number of Christians in Jerusalem would swell to 5000. Biblical scholar, Elmer Towns says, "that eventually about half of the 200,000 people living in Jerusalem were converted to Christ and added to the church."[84]

So, what does this kind of "Yes!" response to God look like in our day? Dr. Kinlaw tells this story: "Josepf Tson, one of the heroes of the faith during the Communist reign in Romania, told me a story about facing the secret police during an interrogation. They were trying to intimidate and destroy him. After a particularly grueling session, he fell

---

[83] Acts 2 MSG
[84] Elmer Towns. Churches that Multiply. Kansas City; Beacon Hill.2003. 51.

on his face before God in desperation and said, "God, they are destroying me. I cannot take any more."

Josepf told me, "I think I heard the voice of God saying to me, 'Josepf, Get up! Who are the secret police compared to the One who sits on the throne of the universe?' "

Josepf got up and returned to the interrogation with a new sense of fear, but it was not fear of his persecutors. Rather, it was a reverence for and holy fear of God himself. One day the chief interrogators said to him, "Josepf, you are stupid, and you will never learn. I guess the only thing we can do is just kill you." Josepf replied, "I understand, sir. That is your ultimate weapon, and when all else has failed, you can kill me. But sir, when you use your ultimate weapon, I will be able to use my ultimate weapon." "What is your ultimate weapon?" demanded the chief mockingly. "Well, you see, your ultimate weapon is to kill me, and my ultimate weapon is to die. When I die, I will be better off than I was before because every sermon I have preached will be sprinkled with my blood."[85]

There is so much power when we have heard the "Whisper" and the direction of the Almighty. Our *Committed Beyond Choice*, "Yes!"! makes it possible.

One of my favorite books is *Why God Used D.L. Moody?*[86] Did the anointing and the "Yes!" apply to this man who preceded Dr. Billy Graham as America's evangelist? His good friend R. A. Torrey said, "The secret of why God used D. L. Moody was that he had a very definite enduement with power from on High, a very clear and definite baptism with the Holy Ghost. Mr. Moody knew he had "the baptism with the Holy Ghost," he had no doubt about it.

In his early days, he was a great hustler, he had a tremendous desire to do something, but he had no real power. He worked very largely in the energy of the flesh. But there were two humble Free Methodist women who used to come over to his meetings in the Y. M. C. A. One was "Auntie Cook" and the other Mrs. Snow. (I think her name

---

[85] Kinlaw, Dennis. *This Day with the Master*. Kindle Edition.
[86] Torrey, R.A. *Why God Used D.L. Moody*. Kindle Edition.

was not Snow at that time.) These two women would come to Mr. Moody at the close of his meetings and say: "We are praying for you." Finally, Mr. Moody became somewhat nettled and said to them one night: "Why are you praying for me? Why don't you pray for the unsaved?" They replied: "We are praying that you may get the power." Mr. Moody did not know what that meant, but he got to thinking about it, and then went to these women and said: "I wish you would tell me what you mean," and they told him about the definite baptism with the Holy Ghost. Then he asked if he might pray with them and not they merely pray for him.

Auntie Cook once told me of the intense fervor with which Mr. Moody prayed on that occasion. She told me in words that I scarcely dare repeat, though I have never forgotten them. And he not only prayed with them, but he also prayed alone.

Not long after, one day on his way to England, he was walking up Wall Street in New York (Mr. Moody very seldom told this, and I almost hesitate to tell it) and in the midst of the bustle and hurry of that city his prayer was answered; the power of God fell upon him as he walked up the street and he had to hurry off to the house of a friend and ask that he might have a room by himself, and in that room, he stayed alone for hours; and the Holy Ghost came upon him filling his soul with such joy that at last he had to ask God to withhold His hand, lest he die on the spot from very joy. He went out from that place with the power of the Holy Ghost upon him, and when he got to London (partly through the prayers of a bedridden saint in Mr. Lessey's church), the power of God wrought through him mightily in North London, and hundreds were added to the churches, and that was what led to his being invited over to the wonderful campaign that followed in later years.

Time and again, Mr. Moody would come to me and say: "Torrey, I want you to preach on the baptism with the Holy Ghost." I do not know how many times he asked me to speak on that subject. Once, when I had been invited to preach in the Fifth Avenue Presbyterian Church, New York (invited at Mr. Moody's suggestion; had it not been for his suggestion, the invitation would never have been extended to me), just before I started for New York, Mr. Moody drove up to my house and said: "Torrey, they want you to preach at the Fifth Avenue Presbyterian Church in New York. It is a great, big church, cost a million dollars to build it." Then he continued: "Torrey, I just want to ask one thing of you. I want to tell you what to preach about. You will preach that sermon of yours on 'Ten Reasons Why I Believe the Bible to be the Word of God' and your sermon on 'The Baptism with the Holy Ghost.'" Time and again, when a call came to me to go off to some church, he would come up to me and say: "Now, Torrey, be sure and preach on the baptism with the Holy Ghost." I do not know how many times he said that to me. Once I asked him: "Mr. Moody, don't you think I have any sermons but those two: 'Ten Reasons Why I Believe the Bible to be the Word of God' and 'The Baptism with the Holy Ghost'?" "Never mind that," he replied, "you give them those two sermons.

Once he had some teachers at Northfield—fine men, all of them, but they did not believe in a definite baptism with the Holy Ghost for the individual. They believed that every child of God was baptized with the Holy Ghost, and they did not believe in any special baptism with the Holy Ghost for the individual. Mr. Moody came to me and said: "Torrey, will you come up to my house after the meeting tonight and I will get those men to come, and I want you to talk this thing out with them."

Of course, I very readily consented, and Mr. Moody and I talked for a long time, but they did not altogether see eye to eye with us. And when they went, Mr. Moody signaled me to remain for a few moments. Mr. Moody sat there with his chin on his breast, as he so often sat when he was in deep thought; then he looked up and said: "Oh, why will they split hairs? Why don't they see that this is just the one thing that they themselves need? They are good teachers, they are wonderful teachers, and I am so glad to have them here, but why will they not see that the baptism with the Holy Ghost is just the one touch that they themselves need?"

"I shall never forget the eighth of July 1894, to my dying day. It was the closing day of the Northfield Students' Conference—the gathering of the students from the eastern colleges. Mr. Moody had asked me to preach on Saturday night and Sunday morning on the baptism with the Holy Ghost. On Saturday night I had spoken about, "The Baptism with the Holy Ghost, What it is, What it does, the Need of it and the Possibility of it." On Sunday morning, I spoke on "The Baptism with the Holy Spirit, How to Get It." It was just exactly twelve o'clock when I finished my morning sermon, and I took out my watch and said: "Mr. Moody has invited us all to go up to the mountain at three o'clock this afternoon to pray for the power of the Holy Spirit. It is three hours to three o'clock. Some of you cannot wait three hours. You do not need to wait. Go to your rooms, go out into the woods, go to your tent, go anywhere where you can get alone with God and have this matter out with Him." At three o'clock, we all gathered in front of Mr. Moody's mother's house (she was then still living), and then began to pass down the lane, through the gate, up on the mountainside. There were four hundred and fifty-six of us in all; I know the number because Paul Moody counted us as we passed through the gate.

After a while, Mr. Moody said: "I don't think we need to go any further; let us sit down here." We sat down on stumps and logs and on the ground. Mr. Moody said: "Have any of you students anything to say?" I think about seventy-five of them arose, one after the other, and said: "Mr. Moody, I could not wait till three o'clock; I have been alone with God since the morning service, and I believe I have a right to say that I have been baptized with the Holy Spirit." When these testimonies were over, Mr. Moody said: "Young men, I can't see any reason why we shouldn't kneel down here right now and ask God that the Holy Ghost may fall upon us just as definitely as He fell upon the apostles on the Day of Pentecost. Let us pray." And we did pray, there on the mountainside. As we had gone up the mountainside heavy clouds had been gathering, and just as we began to pray those clouds broke and the raindrops began to fall through the overhanging pines. But there was another cloud that had been gathering over Northfield for ten days, a cloud big with the mercy and grace and power of God, and as we began to pray our prayers seemed to pierce that cloud and the Holy Ghost fell upon us. Men and women, that is what we all need–the Baptism with the Holy Ghost."[87]

It was America's great evangelist, Dr. Billy Graham 1918-2018, who said, "I am convinced that to be filled with the Spirit is not an option, but a necessity. It is indispensable for an abundant life and for

---

[87] Torrey. Why God Used D.L. Moody.

fruitful service. The Spirit-filled life is not abnormal; it is the normal Christian life. Anything less is subnormal; it is less than what God wants and provides for His children. Therefore, to be filled with the Spirit should never be thought of as an unusual or unique experience for, or known by, only a select few. It is intended for all, needed by all, and available to all. That is why the Scripture commands all of us, 'be filled with the Spirit.' We cannot expect to have the Holy Spirit's fullness in our lives if we are quite content to live without it. Our Father is not likely to entrust this priceless gift to those who are indifferent to its possession. We must, therefore, stir up the gift that is within us by a quiet

Charles G. Finney 1792-1875, America's Greatest Revivalist, described his anointing, "As I turned and was about to take a seat by the fire, I received a mighty baptism of the Holy Ghost.. the Holy Spirit descended upon me in a manner that seemed to go through me, body and soul. I could feel the impression, like a wave of electricity, going through and through me. Indeed, it seemed to come in waves and waves of liquid love, for I could not express it in any other way. It seemed like the very breath of God. I wept aloud with joy and love. I literally bellowed out the unspeakable overflow of my heart. These waves came over me, and over me, and over me, one after the other, until I remember crying out, "I shall die if these waves continue to pass over me." I said, "Lord, I cannot bear anymore," yet I had no fear of death. How long I continued in this state, with this baptism continuing to roll over me and go through me, I do not know. But I know it was late in the evening when a member of my choir—for I was the leader of the choir—came into the office to see me. He was a member of the church. He found me in this state of loud weeping and said to me, "Mr. Finney, what's wrong with you?" I could not answer for some time. He then said, "Are you in pain?" I gathered myself up as best I could and replied, "No, but so happy that I cannot live."[88]

After this anointing and baptism of the Spirit, on many occasions, Finney would just walk in a room, and people would fall under conviction of their sin without him saying a word. The Presence of

---

[88] Finney, Charles G. *The Autobiography of Charles G. Finney* (p. 22). Baker Publishing Group. Kindle Edition.

God was upon him from that day he described he "received a mighty baptism of the Holy Ghost."

Samuel Logan Brengle, Salvation Army, and one of my home state of Indiana's greatest preachers, "The only religion worth having was a "red hot religion" ignited by the unquenchable fire of the Holy Spirit. "What is that fire?" Brengle wrote. "It is love. It is faith. It is hope. It is passion, purpose, determination--utter devotion. It is singleness of eye and a consecration unto death. It is God the Holy Ghost burning in and through a humble, holy, faithful person."

Kinlaw says, "My Methodist friend John R. Church once said, "The first sermon I ever preached had 36 points in it, and when I stood up, I couldn't remember a single one of them. I had to sit down in total humiliation; my mind was a complete blank. It was a little country church in the mountains of North Carolina, and as soon as the service ended, I went running out the door. My father finally caught up with me. He came down the dirt road with his lantern and walked beside me in solemn silence for several minutes. Finally, he said, "Son, God knows you can't preach. I know you can't preach. Now the whole community knows you can't preach. For God's sake, don't put the family through that again." John Church said, "I looked back at him and sobbed, 'Dad, I'm sure that you know I can't preach. I know I can't preach. The church knows I can't preach. But if God knows I can't preach, why doesn't he take the burden off me? Dad, I've got to preach!" And preach he did. He became one of the most effective evangelists in this country. John's ministry was marked by power and fruitfulness. Why? Because he was not preaching for the church or for its people. He was serving God. [89]

I found myself standing in the office of the college President. I felt I was interrupting my friend, Dr. Norman Bridges, then President of Barclay College, later Bethel University. He was fumbling with his cassette recorder, and I asked what he was listening to. "I am listening to one of my favorite preachers, John R. Church. He is so eloquent." "He was one of my dad's favorite preachers," I said. Church's father said, "Don't put the family through that again," but his Heavenly Father made him, according to Kinlaw, "one of the most effective evangelists in the

---

[89] Kinlaw, Dennis F.. Preaching in the Spirit . Warner Press Inc.. Kindle Edition.

country," even "eloquent," according yo Dr. Bridges. Fascinating, both accounts by university presidents. Why? John R. Church said "Yes!" to God. He was *Committed Beyond Choice, the choice* of "Yes or No." "Yes" is the only way to be anointed by the Holy Spirit. In this case, "No, I can't preach," but "Yes, I must!"

"Father, I want to know Thee, but my coward heart fears to give up its toys. I cannot part with them without inward bleeding, and I do not try to hide from Thee the terror of the parting. I come trembling, but I do come. Please root from my heart all those things which I have cherished so long, and which have become a very part of my living self, so that Thou mayest enter and dwell there without a rival. Then shalt Thou make the place of Thy feet glorious. Then shall my heart have no need of the sun to shine in it, for Thyself wilt be the light of it, and there shall be no night there. In Jesus' Name, Amen."[90] A. W. Tozer is describing the *Holy Discontent* I believe that preceded this baptism and anointing of the Holy Spirit. The psalmist put it this way, "Search me, O God, and know my heart; test me and know my anxious thoughts. Point out anything in me that offends you and lead me along the path of everlasting life."[91]

---

[90] A. W. Tozer. *The Pursuit of God.* Harrisburg, PA Christian Publications, 1949. P. 31.
[91] Psalm 139: 23-24 NLT

"Then Jesus said to his disciples, "If anyone wants to follow in my footsteps he must give up all right to himself, take up his cross and follow me."[92] "GIVE UP ALL RIGHTS TO HIMSELF, TAKE UP HIS CROSS AND FOLLOW ME." Wow! "Give up all rights to himself," seems un-American. We boast of our rights, big time! Barna says, "So the first perspective to embrace is the fact that your discontent with the manifestations of your faith — your church, your Bible reading, your Christian friends, your relationship with God — is not a sign of weakness. Quite the opposite: it's more likely a sign of the life that

---

[92] Matthew 16:24 Phillips Modern English

needs to burst forth within you."[93] Paul said, "You must have the same attitude that Christ Jesus had. Though he was God, he did not think of equality with God as something to cling to. Instead, he gave up his divine privileges (Superpowers[94]); he took the humble position of a slave and was born as a human being. When he appeared in human form, he humbled himself in obedience to God and died a criminal's death on a cross."[95]

My brother, Pastor Mark Wright, Brandywine Community Church, Greenfield, Indiana, is known to be a congregation that has a weekly lighting of a candle to celebrate someone coming to Christ. This weekly aspect of their worship has gone on for more than a couple of decades as they have celebrated thousands of people coming to Christ. This is the church mentioned earlier in this book where people felt the Presence of the Lord. I asked him to share his experiences with you:

CLEAN AND EMPTY VESSELS
A Young Boy Attracted to the Anointing
By
Mark Wright

` *In grade school, I remember sitting in the church pew of a small country church,*

watching the pastor give his sermon on Sunday. He was full of love and the joy of the

Lord. I kid you not; this preacher actually had a "glow" about Him. I didn't know what

to call it at the time, but now I realize it was the anointing of God on a person's life.

That pastor was my father, Gene Wright.

The year was 1970. I was nine years old, sitting in a church service, listening to students from Asbury College give their testimony of how God's presence invaded their chapel service for 144 continuous

---

[93] Barna, George. Maximum Faith . Kindle Edition
[94] My addition
[95] Philippians 2: 6-8 NLT

hours. As the students shared their testimony, the presence of God began to move in a very powerful way in our church. Many people that day spontaneously got up from their seats and knelt at the altar, with the desire to get right with God. There was great conviction and repentance, and yet there was also an incredible amount of love and joy in the room. My oldest brother, Gary, was one of the Asbury students giving their testimony. It was the first of many services I would witness of God using their lives to impact thousands of others for Christ. Everywhere they would go and share about the Asbury revival, revival would then break out in that church and community! How is it that God used ordinary college students to spread revival and renewal across this Nation and eventually around the world? He simply anointed them to go and to share what they had witnessed!

It was during those same formative grade school years that I was introduced to a Christian recording artist, Dallas Holm. I was no different than other kids who loved listening to rock music on the radio, and yet could not get enough of Dallas' music. I bought every album he recorded. What was it that attracted a young boy to listen for endless hours to songs about the love of God? It was the anointing of God on this singer's life.

What does it mean to be anointed? The anointing is the power of God at work in you. It is the supernatural ability from God that enables you to do things that you are not capable of doing in your own strength. It's about God power working in your life. "The kingdom of God does not consist in talk but in power." 1 Corinthians 4:20

Vessels Used by God

As I began to grow in my walk with the Lord, I came to realize that God is no respecter of persons. This same anointing I was so attracted to as a boy is available to every Christ-follower! The Word of God declares…"You shall receive power when the Holy Spirit has come upon you, and you shall be witnesses to Me in Jerusalem, and in all Judea and Samaria, and to the end of the earth" Acts 1:8 NLT.

Have you ever wondered how you can experience God's anointing on your life? The secret is found in a pure and surrendered life. The Bible refers to us who are believers as being human vessels used by God for

111

His purpose. We are containers, meant to carry God's power and anointing within our own lives, so we can make a difference in the world we live in.

Clean Vessels

God will use any vessel, but it must be clean. He will not pour His clean Holy Spirit into dirty, unholy vessels. God pours His oil into clean vessels. Therefore, if anyone cleanses himself from what is dishonorable, he will be a vessel for honorable use, set apart as holy, useful to the master of the house, ready for every good work. 2 Timothy 2:21 (ESV)

When we to turn from sin and endeavor to live our lives in the way of the Lord, it's then that God gives us clean and pure hearts. "I have kept my heart pure; I am clean and without sin?" Proverbs 20:9

Another word for pure is holy. The Bible says those with a holy heart are the ones who receive God's blessing and anointing on their lives. "Who may ascend the mountain of the Lord? Who may stand in his holy place? The one who has clean hands and a pure heart, who does not trust in an idol or swear by a false god. They will receive blessing from the Lord." Psalm. 24:3-5

Empty Vessels

God will use any vessel, but it must be clean and empty. Many people say they want to be used of God and to be anointed, but they don't realize that there is a price to pay. The price of the anointing is to empty ourselves of our wishes, desires, personal, preferences, and aspirations, and to fully surrender ourselves to God's will. We don't die to self easily because we think what we're giving up is too costly. Thinking my life will no longer be enjoyable, but not realizing that the most enjoyable and fulfilling life we could ever live comes only when I fully surrender to the will of God. Jesus said…"If any of you wants to be my follower, you must give up your own way, take up your cross daily, and follow me. if you try to hang on to your life, you will lose it. But if you give up your life for my sake, you will save it." Luke 9:23-24 (NLT)

A Fulfilling Life

The most fulfilling life is a fruitful one used by God. I love the following quote from

Max Lucado: "When you're full of yourself, God can't fill you. But when you empty yourself, God

has a useful vessel." ~ Max Lucado

Throughout Scripture, we are called to surrender our lives to God and to be continually filled with the Holy Spirit. Of course, every Christian receives the Holy Spirit upon conversion, but just like the same people received repeated fillings of the Spirit in the book of Acts, we also need to be filled repeatedly. If we are not being continually filled with the Holy Spirit, we are not going to have the strength and power to accomplish God's purposes for our lives. In Galatians, Paul says that the Spirit produces fruit within that cannot be produced otherwise:

"But the fruit of the Spirit is love, joy, peace, patience, kindness, goodness, faithfulness,

gentleness, self-control; against such things, there is no law" Galatians 5:22-23 (ESV).

Every single day I have to pray, "God, empty me of me and fill me with your Spirit." I must be willing to give up what my flesh desires and let the Spirit take control, otherwise I can do nothing. At least nothing of true value. Why has my attraction to the anointing not waned over the years? Because I'm convinced that a life lived as a vessel of the Holy Spirit, fully surrendered to the will of God, is truly the most fulfilling and incredible life.

Daily Prayer

Father, I surrender to You today. I willingly submit to Your will. Give me a clean heart. Give me a heart filled with clean thoughts and right desires. Empty me of me and to fill me with Your Holy Spirit. I desire to be in close communion with You all day long. Anoint me and give me Your strength and power so that my life will reflect You, then I'll be able to love others the way You love them. Guide my steps and make my life fruitful for You. I pray this in Your name, Jesus. Amen.

Pastor Mark Wright

Brandywine Community Church

I was at a conference in northern Indiana. It is Amish country. We stopped at a bakery and ordered a Carmel/Cinnamon donut. I cannot really describe the delicious taste I experienced. My vocabulary to describe this food fails me, and I can only say it is something "Other" in the cuisine realm. As I decided to explain this to you, this week, that donut was proclaimed the best donut in the United States just this past week![96] Nevertheless, I know something that is sweeter. I certainly have no words for Him either. "Not only is our God one who provides honey for his people in the wilderness, sweetness in the midst of our grueling times, but his words are "sweeter also than honey and drippings of the honeycomb" Psalm 19:10 KJV. "How sweet are your words to my taste, sweeter than honey to my mouth." Psalm 119:103 KJV. Truly, this is "none like Him."

Reflection and Discussion Questions

1. What is then most important element of the opening story, "Folks God is here" told by Kinlaw in this chapter?
2. Several "anointed leaders describe their spiritual baptism in this chapter. What did you learn or observe from Cowman, Moody, Josepf Tson, Finney, Graham, Church, Tozer or Mark Wright?
3. What is the most important status of the heart in order to be "anointed" by the Holy Spirit?
4. How do you see lives changed by this anointing in these last two chapters?
5. Close in praying for your group and again for your 3rd chair loved ones.

Notes

_____

_____

_____

_____

---

[96] https://fox59.com/indiana-news/americas-greatest-donuts-indiana-bakery-gobbles-up-competition/

Chapter Nine
He Just Kept On Loving Me

Now that I am old and gray, do not abandon me, O God. Let me proclaim your power to this new generation, your mighty miracles to all who come after me. Psalm 71:17-18. NLT

Imagine with me a rock and limestone island in the deep blue sea. The distant figure on the brown volcanic lava rock and mostly treeless ridges staring out to the distant shore is an elderly man. His silver hair and beard are gently tossed by the sea breeze. His Jewish skin was bronzed by the sun. His clothing is that of Jesus' day. If you got closer to him and peered into his brown Jewish eyes you might think he was sick. Indeed, the old man is sad and homesick for those on the distant shore. On clear days he could see that beckoning distant shore, about 40 miles. It was where family and friends resided along with evidence of his lifetime of love and labor.

The old gentleman smiled as he thought of the faces of his loved ones. He knew what they were doing...really what he was doing. It was the Lord's Day, Sunday, and he was doing what godly men do on the Lord's Day. He thought of his dear friend Jesus; he could hear His voice in his mind as he recalled the," Follow Me, and I will make you Fishers of men." He and his brother had left their dad with their hired hands standing in the fishing boats. It was an entire lifetime ago now, yet seemed like yesterday.

He lifted his arms and hands in praise and maybe sang a hymn, a Psalm, first sung by King David. I canalmost hear him sing, "Let all that I praise the Lord; with my whole heart, I will praise his holy name. Let all that I am praise the Lord; may I never forget the good things he does for me. He forgives all my sins and heals all my diseases. He redeems me from death and crowns me with love and tender mercies. He fills my life with good things."[97]

I am sure tears filled his eyes as he recalled how loved and special Jesus always made him feel. Peace flooded his heart, even on this island of punishment and imprisonment, because of his witness for Jesus.

As he worshipped, he heard the most beautiful music behind him. He turned to see the source of the heavenly Voice and music. But as he turned, he looked straight into the face of God Himself. What does a Godly man do when he looks into the face of God? I am sure I do not know. However, this elderly gentleman fell as if dead. He fainted. Then there was an outstretched nail-scarred hand and a comforting, familiar voice, and John said, "I saw this and fainted dead at his feet. His right hand pulled me upright; His voice reassured me: "Don't fear I am First, I am Last, I'm Alive. I died, but I came to life, and my life is now forever. See these keys in my hand? They open and lock Death's doors; they open and lock Hell's gates. Now write down everything you see."[98] "And John told everything he saw: God's Word—the witness of Jesus Christ!"[99]

What an opening scene to the 66th and final book of the Bible! Revelation, a book that promises, "Blessed is the one who reads aloud the words of this prophecy, and blessed are those who hear it and take to heart what is written in it,"[100] The Apostle John, the last living Apostle said, "I, John, your brother and companion in the suffering and kingdom and patient endurance that are ours in Jesus, was on the island of Patmos because of the word of God and the testimony of Jesus. On the Lord's Day, I was in the Spirit, and I heard behind me a loud voice like a trumpet, which said: "Write on a scroll what you see and send it to the seven churches: to Ephesus, Smyrna, Pergamum, Thyatira, Sardis, Philadelphia and Laodicea."[101] The aged Apostle nearing the century mark wrote the Revelation circa '90s.[102]

---

[97] Psalm 103. NLT

[98] Revelations 1: 17-18 MSG.

[99] Revelation 1 MSG

[100] Revelation 1 NIV

[101] Ibid.

[102] Paul Hoskins. *WHY AND WHEN DID JOHN WRITE REVELATION?*.2020. https://exegeticaltools.com/2020/05/24/why-and-when-did-john-write-revelation/ Irenaeus claims that John saw the visions of Revelation at the end

Thinking of the Apostle John, have you noticed how Jesus, God, re-names people in the Bible? In the Old Testament, God changes Abram to Abraham, Jacob to Israel. In the New Testament, the first book is Matthew, "Gift of God," from the original Levi. The names seem descriptive of what God is going to change them into. "Abram means exalted father, and Abraham means father of a multitude. Both names represent what was possible for Abraham to become because of the covenant."[103] Simon, the fisherman, becomes "(Simeon in Hebrew), meaning "The one who hears (Word of God)," and Peter (Chepas in Hebrew) means "a rock." The name changes is to underline the transformation of the person whom hear words of God to a spiritual rock."[104]

What was the nickname Jesus gave John and his brother James? "James, son of Zebedee and his brother John (to them he gave the name Boanerges, which means "sons of thunder").[105] Why did Jesus call them "Sons of Thunder" or "Thunderbolts"? Can you think of any occasions in the Gospels where they earned such bold and fiery labels?

One such occasion may have included their mother, Salome. "Then the mother of James and John, the sons of Zebedee, came to Jesus with her sons. She knelt respectfully to ask a favor. "What is your request?" he asked. (I think Jesus smiled here; He knew this was going to be a good one.) She replied, "In your Kingdom, please let my two sons sit in places of honor next to you, one on your right and the other on your left." But Jesus answered by saying to them, "You don't know what you are asking! Are you able to drink from the bitter cup of suffering I am about to drink?" "Oh yes," they replied, "we are able!" Yea, right? What nerve by the brothers and momma! "Oh yes! We are able!" Yep, "Thunderbolts!"

---

of Domitian's reign. This would place the book somewhere in the 90's, since Domitian's reign ended in A.D. 9.
[103]
https://www.google.com/search?q=abram+to+abraham+meaning&rlz=1C1SQJ L_enUS905US905&oq=Abram+to+Abraham&aqs=chrome.3.0i355i512j46i512j0 i512l6j0i390i650l2.15702j0j15&sourceid=chrome&ie=UTF-8
[104] https://effendy-arifin.medium.com/why-was-simons-name-changed-to-peter-cc7bfa19bcc2
[105] Mark 3:17 NIV

Yes, and their request caused trouble. "When the ten other disciples heard what James and John had asked, they were indignant. "But Jesus called them together," small group discussion time.

On another occasion, after the Mt. of Transfiguration in Mark 9, the disciples did not have the spiritual strength to cast a demon out of a boy, even though earlier they had done so. Then Jesus caught them arguing about who was the most spiritual. John follows this up with, "Hey Jesus, we did something right today, "We saw someone using your name to cast out demons, but we told him to stop because he wasn't in our group." At this point, I see Jesus rub His forehead and say, "Don't stop him!" Jesus said. "No one who performs a miracle in my name will soon be able to speak evil of me. Anyone, who is not against us, is for us." Earlier in this chapter, He said, "You faithless people! How long must I be with you? How long must I put up with you?"[106] I am sure He has said the same about me to the angels.

However, the most iconic "Sons of Thunder" moment may have been when Jesus and the disciples were headed across Samaria to Jerusalem, and Jesus sent some of the group ahead to secure lodging and food. However, there were racial problems between the Samaritans and the Jews. "But the people of the village did not welcome Jesus."[107] "When the disciples James and John saw this, they said, "Lord, do you want us to call fire down from heaven to destroy them?" Jesus turned and rebuked them. Then Jesus and his disciples went on to another village."[108] It's obvious James and John really wanted to turn the Samaritans into Crispy Critters for sure. Yep, "Thunderbolts," "Sons of Thunder," for sure!

Yet, by the end of John's life, he acquired another nickname. "Despite this strong, demanding, fiery, impetuous aspect of the brothers' nature, John was later known not as a "son of thunder," but as the "apostle of love" for his promotion of outgoing love as a godly attribute."[109] How did this happen? How do you go from a "Son of

---

[106] Mark 9 NLT
[107] Luke 9 NLT.
[108] Luke 9 GNT
[109] David Hulme. *"Son of Thunder, Apostle of Love."* 2009.
https://www.vision.org/apostles-part-16-son-of-thunder-apostle-of-love-688

Thunder" to an "Apostle of Love"? Can a person change that much? How did he change? What happened?

Let's look at John's Gospel for clues. John had about sixty years to consider how to describe his time with Jesus.[110] John closes his Gospel by saying, "Now, there are many other things that Jesus did. If they were all written down one by one, I suppose that the whole world could not hold the books that would be written."[111] Sixty years of looking back! He is the last living Apostle. He needs to preserve for all of us what he saw, heard, and experienced. His closing statement points to a process of elimination to what is most important.

Have you ever noticed he doesn't call himself "John" in his Gospel or "I, John" as he did in Revelation? What does he call himself? You may remember he calls himself "the disciple whom Jesus loved" (John 13:23; 19:26; 20:2; 21:20). Some have speculated that John was saying in some way, "I'm special, Jesus loved me more than anyone else." Remember, we do see the disciples in Mark 6 arguing over who among them is the greatest. Actually, John uses a verb tense that usually implies a process – saying the disciple whom Jesus _was_ loving." The implication is, "He **kept** on loving me and loving me and loving me." Do not think of John as some kind of soft, sentimental, wishy-washy weakling. He was a "son of thunder". And now, writing many years later at the end of his long life, he has one chance to describe himself to his audience. He could have done this in several different ways, each with its own emphasis."[112] So how does John describe himself? "I am the disciple that Jesus just kept on loving." It's a confession. A confession of a man looking back over his whole life! John is thinking of his relationship with Jesus when Jesus was physically in person with him; he's thinking of these last years with Jesus in person spiritually. "I'm the one He just never gave up on. He just kept loving me!"

[110]Bill Creasy. Logos Bible Study. *The Gospel of John*. 2021. The Gospel According to John operates outside this "synoptic tradition." Most scholars place the gospel's composition somewhere between A.D. 90-100, w
[111] John 21 GNT
[112] David Alan Black. *The Disciple Whom Jesus Kept On Loving*. https://www.daveblackonline.com/disciple_whom_jesus_kept_on_lovi.htm

Therefore, that one phrase repeated four times in John's Gospel gives us a strong indication of the transforming love of God to a "Son of Thunder."

John was younger than Jesus and the other disciples, who were all about the same age as Jesus. It appears that young John, alone, sensed the seriousness of the hour at the last supper meal. Peterson translates that John "was reclining against him, his head on his shoulder," others say he was leaning on Jesus' chest. While Jesus loved John, John was loving Jesus back.

John came from a well-respected Jewish family. The family had hired workers in the fishing business, which showed their wealth as well. They were a deeply Jewish family with influence. Notice in his Gospel he tells us that after initially fleeing the arrest scene in the garden, he gained entrance into Caiaphas' courtyard to come alongside Jesus. He lets his friend, Simon Peter, into the courtyard too. In John's own words he, "was acquainted with the high priest, so he was allowed to enter the high priest's courtyard with Jesus. Peter had to stay outside the gate. Then the disciple who knew the high priest spoke to the woman watching at the gate, and she let Peter in."[113]

That means John witnessed all that happened to Jesus at Caiaphas' house. He became an eyewitness to the awful, ugly scene. "then they were spitting in his face and knocking him around. They jeered as they slapped him: "Prophesy, Messiah: Who hit you that time?"[114] Young John stayed at Jesus' side during the interrogation by Annas, then the High Priest Caiaphas. That's what you do when someone you love is going through bad stuff. You are there with them. You love them; you are willing to take risks to be with them. Only John was there; the other disciples were not; Peter tried. Only John stood with Jesus. The disciple Jesus kept on loving "kept on loving" kept Jesus too. While others fled, he made his choice. I believe this is a defining moment for the young disciple, Jesus' follower.

There is a moving scene told by John at the cross. "While the soldiers were looking after themselves, Jesus' mother, his aunt (John's

---

113 John 18 NLT
114 Matthew 26 MSG

mother Salome), Mary, the wife of Clopas, and Mary Magdalene stood at the foot of the cross. Jesus saw his mother and the disciple he loved standing near her. He said to his mother, "Woman, here is your son." Then to the disciple, "Here is your mother." From that moment, the disciple accepted her as his own mother."[115] This is interesting. Jesus puts John in charge of caring and replacing him in caring for His mother. Jesus trusts John with his mother. John says he "accepted her as his own mother." Historians of the church tell us John did just that. Early church fathers say John cared for Mary until her death building a house for her in Ephesus, where he was headquartered in ministry. The key word here is "love."

John's conclusion towards the end of his long life is, "God is love." He went on to say that we should love each other as Jesus loved and "kept on loving him." "My dear, dear friends, if God loved us like this, we certainly ought to love each other. No one has seen God, ever. But if we love one another, God dwells deeply within us, and his love becomes complete in us—perfect love!"[116] I believe that the transforming love of Jesus points back to the interrogation of Jesus at Caiaphas courtyard. John loving Jesus back, saved, and transformed, his own life, who he was. He lived the rest of his life being molded and shaped by that continuing process of divine love.

One of the most interesting stories about how this looked in John's life is not in the Bible. The story is told by Clement of Alexandria records the account of John at the end of his writing, "Who is the Rich Man that Shall Be Saved"? (Ante-Nicene Fathers, Vol. 2, Clement, XLII). Clement notes that the account is "not a (fictional) tale but a narrative handed down and committed to the custody of memory about the Apostle John." After John's exile to Patmos, he returned to Ephesus[117]. (Further explanation.) [118]

---

[115] John 19 MSG

[116] 1 John 4 MSG

[117] https://matthewfretwell.com/2022/07/11/the-apostle-john-a-discipleship-example-of-rescue-restoration/

[118] MacArthur, John F.. 1, 2, 3 John and Jude (MacArthur Bible Studies) (p. 2). Harper Christian Resources. Kindle Edition. The church Fathers (e.g., Justin Martyr, Irenaeus, Clement of Alexandria, Eusebius) indicate that after that time, John lived at Ephesus in Asia Minor, carrying out an extensive evangelistic

"He (John) returned to Ephesus from the isle of Patmos, he went away, being invited, to the contiguous territories of the nations, here to appoint bishops, there to set in order whole Churches, there to ordain such as were marked out by the Spirit.

Having come to one of the cities not far off (the name of which some give) and having put the brethren to rest in other matters, at last, looking to the bishop appointed, and seeing a youth, powerful in body, comely in appearance, and ardent, said, "This (youth) I commit to you in all earnestness, in the presence of the Church, and with Christ as witness." (You are to mentor and disciple, train him.) And on his accepting and promising all, he gave the same injunction and testimony. And he set out for Ephesus.

And the presbyter taking home the youth committed to him, reared, kept, cherished, and finally baptized him. After this he relaxed his stricter care and guardianship, under the idea that the seal of the Lord he had set on him was a complete protection to him.

But on his obtaining premature freedom, some youths of his age, idle, dissolute, and adepts in evil courses, corrupt him. First they entice him by many costly entertainments; then afterwards by night issuing forth for highway robbery, they take him along with them. Then, they dared to execute together something greater. And he by degrees got accustomed; and from greatness of nature, when he had gone aside from the right path, and like a hard-mouthed and powerful horse, had taken the bit between his teeth, rushed with all the more force down into the depths. *And having*

---

program, overseeing many of the churches that had arisen, and conducting an extensive writing ministry (e.g., epistles, the gospel of John, and Revelation). One church Father (Papias), who had direct contact with John, described him as a "living and abiding voice." As the last remaining apostle, John's testimony was highly authoritative among the churches.

entirely despaired of salvation in God, he no longer meditated what was insignificant, but having perpetrated some great exploit, now that he was once lost, he made up his mind to a like fate with the rest. Taking them and forming a band of robbers, **he was the prompt captain of the bandits, the fiercest, the bloodiest, the cruelest.**

Time passed, and some necessity having emerged, they sent again for John. He, when he had settled the other matters on account of which he came, said, "Come now, "O bishop, restore to us the deposit which I and the Savior committed to you in the face of the Church over which you preside, as witness." The other was at first confounded, thinking that it was a false charge about money which he did not get; and he could neither believe the allegation regarding what he had not, nor disbelieve John. But when he said, "I demand the young man, and the soul of the brother," the old man, groaning deeply, and bursting into tears, said, "He is dead." "How and what kind of death?" the Apostle asked. "He is dead," he said, "to God. For he turned wicked and abandoned, and at last a robber; and now he has taken possession of the mountain in front of the church, along with a band like him."

Rending, therefore, his clothes, and striking his head with great lamentation, the apostle said, "It was a fine guard of a brother's soul I left! But let a horse be brought me and let someone be my guide on the way."

He rode away, just as he was, straight from the church. On coming to the place, he is arrested by the robbers' outpost; neither fleeing nor entreating, but crying, "It was for this I came. Lead me to your captain." Who, meanwhile, was waiting, all armed as he was. But when he recognized John as he advanced, he turned, ashamed, took flight. The other(the old Apostle John) followed with all his might, forgetting his age, crying,

"Why, my son, do you flee from me, your father, unarmed, old? Son, pity me. Fear not; you still have hope of life. I will give account to Christ for you. If need be, I will willingly endure your death, as the Lord did death for us. For you I will surrender my life. Stand, believe; Christ has sent me."

And he, when he heard, first stood, looking down; then threw down his arms, then trembled and wept bitterly. And on the old man approaching, he embraced him, speaking for himself with lamentations as he could, and baptized a second time with tears, concealing only his right hand. The other, pledging, and assuring him on oath that he would find forgiveness for himself from the Savior, beseeching and falling on his knees, and kissing his right hand itself, as now purified by repentance, led him back to the church.

Then by supplicating with copious prayers, and striving along with him in continual fasting, and subduing his mind by various utterances of words, did not depart, as they say, till he restored him to the Church."

Oh, my! The old Apostle John, whom Jesus described as the "Son of Thunder," is loving and "kept on loving" another Son of Thunder who had strayed so far from God, "he was the prompt captain of the bandits, the fiercest, the bloodiest, the cruelest." The aged Apostle, probably in his 90's, is willing to stand in punishment for the boy. "Fear not; you still have hope of life. I will give account to Christ for you. If need be, I will willingly endure your death, as the Lord did death for us. For you, I will surrender my life. Stand, believe; Christ has sent me." It is not a surprise to me that the young bandit "threw down his arms, then trembled and wept bitterly." John brought him back to Christ and the church. John said, "My beloved friends, let us continue to love each other since love comes from God. Everyone who loves is born of God and experiences a relationship with God. The person who refuses to love doesn't

125

know the first thing about God because God is love—so you can't know him if you don't love. This is how God showed his love for us: God sent his only Son into the world so we might live through him. This is the kind of love we are talking about— not that we once upon a time loved God, but that he loved us and sent his Son as a sacrifice to clear away our sins and the damage they've done to our relationship with God."[119] This love of God, Jesus, that "kept" loving John changed and matured him he said, "God is love. When we take up permanent residence in a life of love, we live in God, and God lives in us. This way, love has the run of the house, becomes at home and mature in us."

So, there you have it. John, Son of Thunder, confesses that he was someone Jesus "kept on loving." That love changed and matured him to the point that he loved others and became the "Apostle of Love." When this "Jesus' love" is given "the run of the house" of our heart, "becomes at home" it will transform and "mature us." We become like Jesus. We become an "Apostle of Love."

Somehow, I can't help but imagine a conversation in heaven between the Father, Son, and the Holy Spirit. The Father says, "We still need someone to write book 66. Who can We trust with that Revelation?" I hear Jesus say, "I have just the guy for it! Father, he is quite busy with the work of our church; he will need quiet and isolation." "Has he given Us permission to use his life as needed? Is He totally committed to Us?" the Father asked. The Spirit says, "Oh, Yes! Committed Beyond Choice. He wants and is eager for Us to use, and spend, his life anyway, anywhere, for any purpose. We choose. His answer has been, "Yes!" for a long time."

Soon, I hear horse hoofs beating the cobblestone streets of Ephesus as Roman Emperor Titus Flavius Domitianus's (circa 95 AC.) troops take the old preacher, Bishop, as a prisoner. Because of the crack-down on the Christians and his witness for Christ, he is banished to the island of

---

[119] 1 John 4 MSG

126

Patmos. Sunday comes, and the old Bishop peers out across the blue Aegean Sea toward his hometown of Ephesus. And then it happens, "Don't be afraid. Get up off the ground. Write everything you see and hear."

Reflection and Discussion Questions

1. Describe John and James "Sons of Thunder" character and personality traits that led to their nickname from Jesus.
2. How would you describe the process of John "Son of Thunder" to becoming the "Apostle of Love."
3. Describe Jesus' "Kept on Loving" confession of John.
4. What is the most important thing you learned in this chapter? Why is it important?
5. Which story of Jesus training his disciples is your favorite? Why?
6. What is a challenge to living a "Yes Lord" lifestyle? Why?
7. What is a blessing to living a "Yes Lord" lifestyle? Why?
8. What is one thing you will remember about this "Yes, committed beyond Choice" study? Why?
9. Close in praying for your group and again for your 3rd chair loved ones.

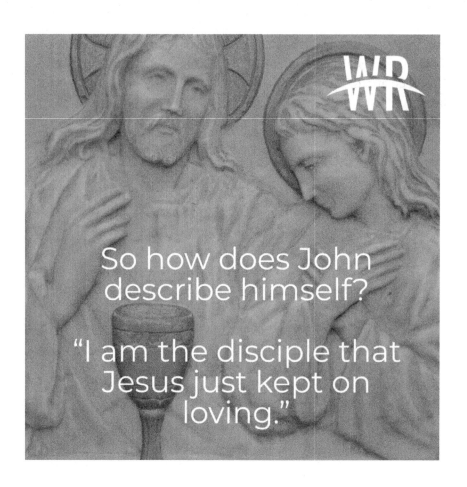

So how does John describe himself?

"I am the disciple that Jesus just kept on loving."

Notes

_____
_____
_____
_____
_____
_____
_____
_____
_____
_____
_____
_____

Made in the USA
Middletown, DE
09 September 2023

37770009R00076